200
Stitch Patterns
for Baby Blankets

Jan Eaton

Search Press

A QUARTO BOOK

Published in 2018 by
Search Press Ltd
Wellwood
North Farm Road
Tunbridge Wells
Kent TN2 3DR

ISBN: 978-1-78221-634-6

Conceived, edited and designed by
Quarto Publishing
an imrint of The Quarto Group
The Old Brewery
6 Blundell Street
London N7 9BH
www.quartoknows.com

QUAR.SPBB2

Senior Editor Liz Pasfield
Art Editor and Designer Julie Francis
Assistant Art Director Penny Cobb
Pattern Checkers Eva Yates, Helen Jordan
Copy Editor Claire Waite Brown
Photographers Paul Forrester,
Phil Wilkins
Illustrators Coral Mula, Kuo Kang Chen

Art Director Moira Clinch
Publisher Paul Carslake

Printed in China

Contents

Key	KNITTED
	CROCHET

Block and Stitch Directory   16

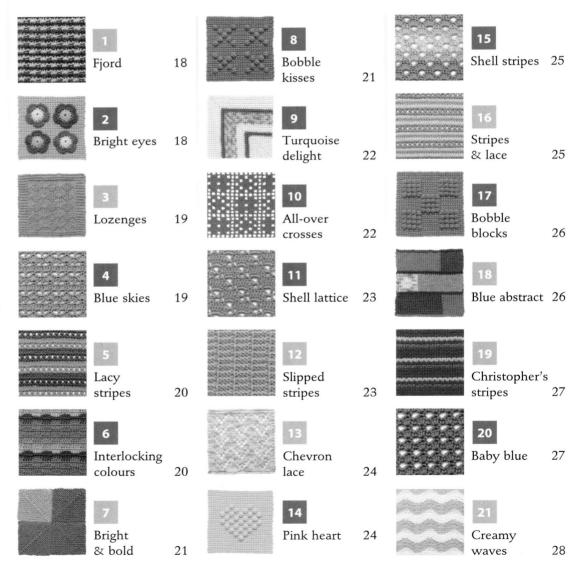

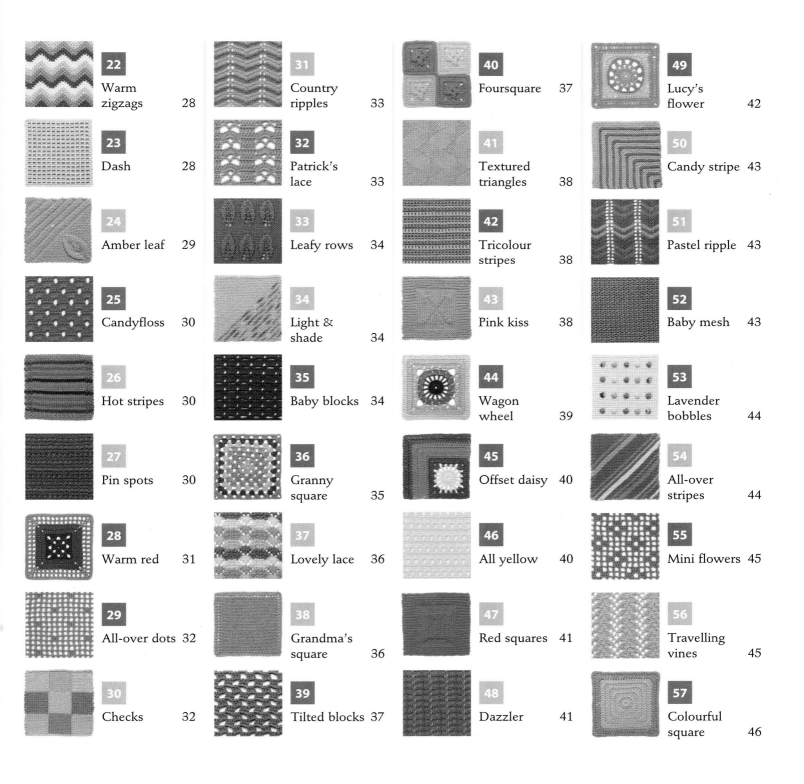

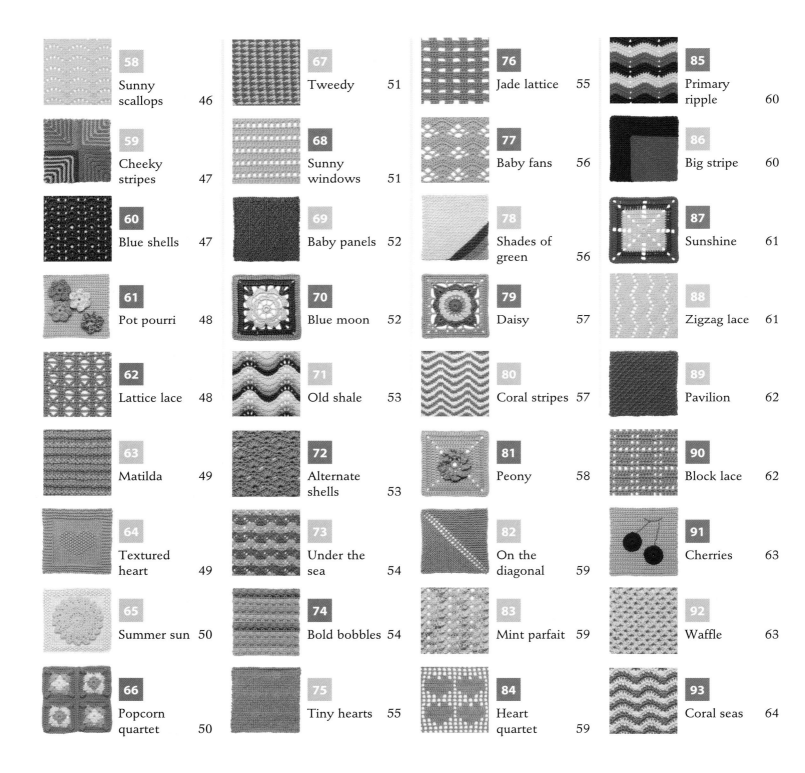

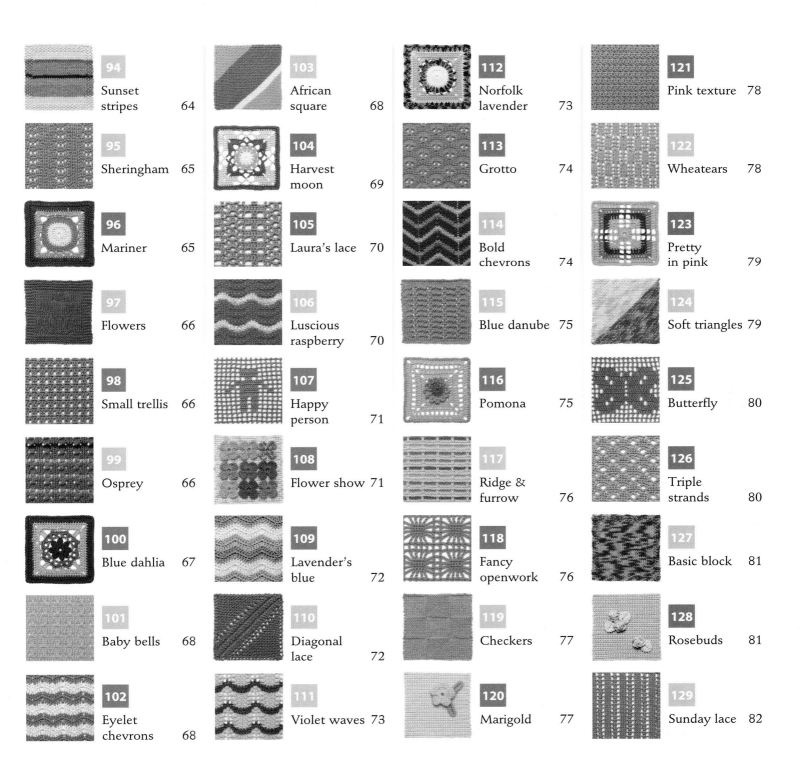

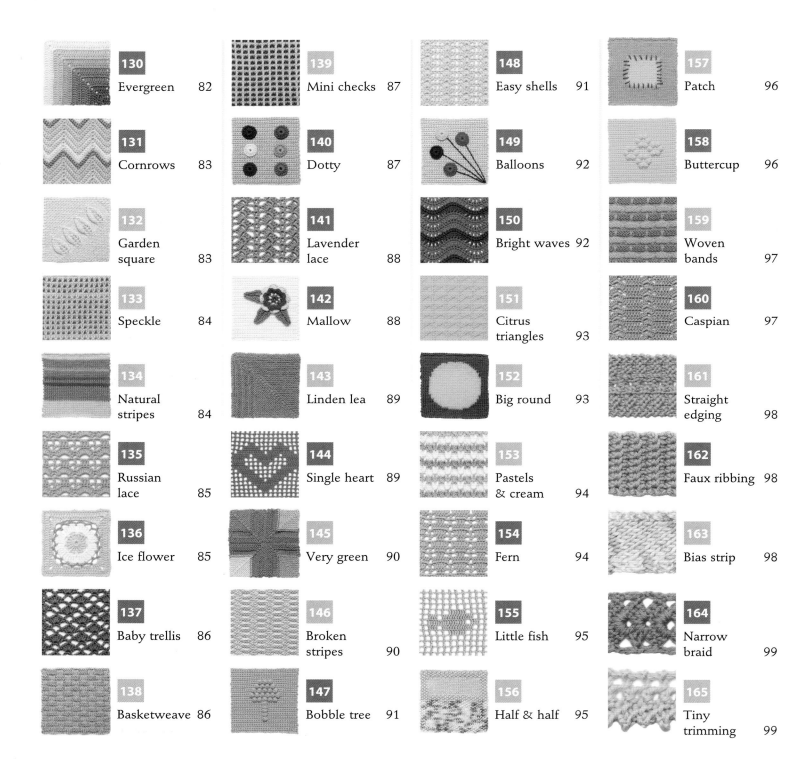

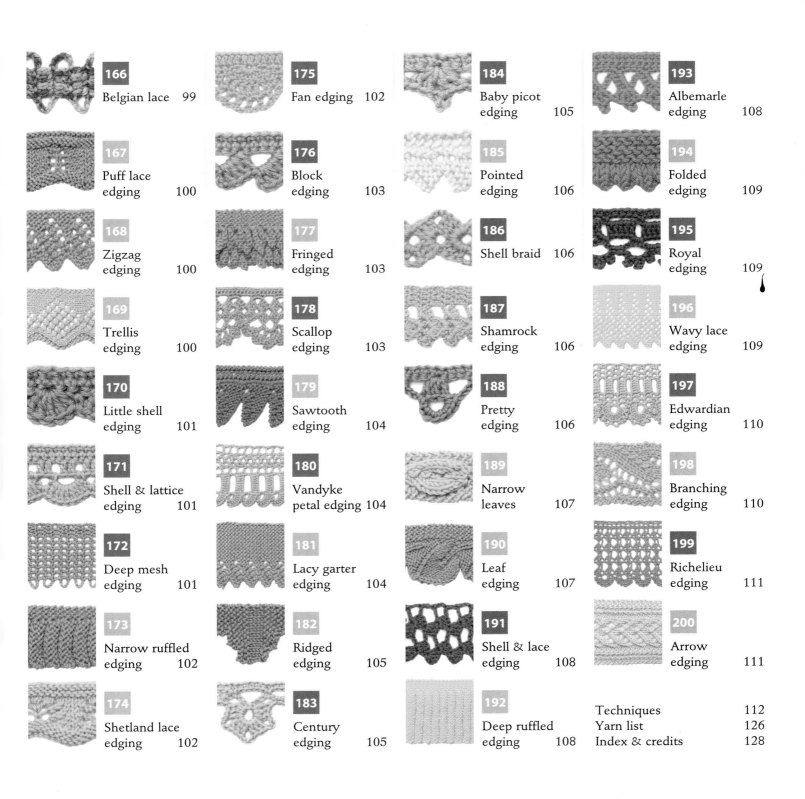

Introduction

Crochet and knitting are both popular pastimes, and many crafters are familiar with either way of manipulating yarn, with hook or needles, to make wonderful fabrics. Baby blankets, shawls and afghans are ever popular items to make, whether assembled from blocks or worked in a single piece, and make the perfect gift for friends and family.

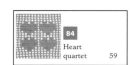

The 200 blocks, stitch patterns and edgings in this book, each one with complete instructions and colour photography, have been carefully designed to help even the novice crafter create fabulous, colourful items for babies from newborn to toddler. Encompassing both traditional crochet and knit patterns and brand new designs, this book will inspire both new and experienced crafters to take up the challenge of working with and combining a comprehensive palette of colours and yarns to make wonderful blankets, afghans and shawls for their own child, or to give as gifts. Each entry in the directory is cross-referenced by symbols describing the techniques used and the degree of difficulty of the pattern, from beginner to advanced, and suggestions are given for mixing and matching blocks and working stitch patterns in various colour combinations. Also included is a useful refresher course of crochet and knitting stitches and techniques. From working the basic stitches through to joining blocks and attaching an edging, each technique is illustrated with clear, easy-to-follow diagrams backed up with informative text that helps you to understand each step.

How to use this book

Contents

The illustrated contents list includes photographs of all the blocks, stitch patterns and edgings featured in the book, accompanied by their name, swatch number and the page the pattern can be found on. The preliminary pages give advice on choosing and using yarns, exploring the world of colour, and experimenting with blocks and stitch patterns.

The block and stitch directory

The directory is where you will find the blocks, stitch patterns and edgings to knit and crochet. There is a colour photograph of each swatch, accompanied by a symbol indicating which technique is used in the pattern, plus one that indicates the degree of difficulty of that particular pattern. Yarn colours are shown as numbers within round symbols, and each number refers to an actual yarn, as detailed on pages 126–127.

Edgings

At the end of the directory there are patterns for knitted and crochet edgings, any of which can be used to finish off your baby blanket with style.

Techniques

The final section of the book contains a short refresher course on working both knitting and crochet techniques.

Yarns used

At the end of the techniques section there is a list of the actual yarns from the colour palette used to work the patterns in the directory.

7 ORANGE *Jaeger* SWATCHES 36, 59, 66, 103
Matchmaker DK, shade 898

Using the block and stitch directory

The blocks
Blocks are worked over a set number of stitches. The complete block is shown in the photograph.

Numbering
Each block or stitch pattern is numbered.

A light tint indicates a knitting pattern or block.

A dark tint is a crochet pattern or block.

The stitch patterns
Stitch patterns are worked over a multiple of stitches. A section of the swatch is shown in the photograph.

Instructions
Full instructions are given for each swatch.

Yarns
There is a yarn key for each swatch. Match the numbers to the yarn list on pages 126–127.

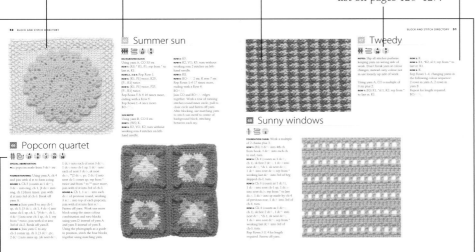

Understanding the symbols
Each sample is accompanied by a symbol indicating if the sample is a crochet or knitting pattern and the pattern's degree of difficulty, and one or more symbols indicating how each pattern is worked.

LEVEL OF DIFFICULTY

 Easy crochet

 Some crochet experience required

 Challenging crochet

 Easy knitting

 Some knitting experience required

 Challenging knitting

METHOD OF WORKING

 Block or stitch pattern worked in horizontal rows

 Block worked in rounds

 Block worked in diagonal rows

 Edging worked widthways

 Edging worked lengthways

 Block worked in L-shaped rows

 Filet crochet

Reading the patterns

American/*English* terminology
The names of some stitches and technical terms differ in the US and the UK (see page 128). The patterns in this book are written using dual terminology, with the US first followed by the UK in grey italic. For example, '1 sc/*dc* into next tr/*dtr*' equates to '1 sc into next tr' using US terminology and '1 dc into next dtr' using UK terminology. Use one system or the other; don't try to swap between the two.

Abbreviations

alt	alternate	rem	remaining
BO/*CO*	bind/*cast* off	rep	repeat
beg	beginning	RS	right side
ch(s)	chain(s)	sc/*dc*	single/*double*
CO	cast on		crochet
cont	continue	sk	skip
dc/*tr*	double/*treble*	sl	slip
	crochet	sl st	slip stitch
dec	decrease	sp(s)	space(s)
foll	following	ssk	slip, slip,
hdc/*htr*	half double/		knit
	treble crochet	st(s)	stitch(es)
inc	increase	tbl	through
K	knit		back loops
K2tog	knit 2	tog	together
	together	tr/*dtr*	treble/*double*
P	purl		*treble* crochet
P2tog	purl 2	WS	wrong side
	together	wyib	with yarn
patt	pattern		in back
psso	pass slipped	wyif	with yarn
	stitch over		in front
p2sso	pass 2	YO	yarn over
	slipped		
	stitches over		

Useful yarn/hook combinations
4ply or sport weight: 2.5–3.5mm (US sizes B–E)
Double knitting (DK): 3.5–4.5mm (US sizes E–G)
Aran or worsted weight: 5–6mm (US sizes I–J)

Useful yarn/needle combinations
4ply or sport weight: 2.5–3.5mm (US sizes 2–4)
Double knitting (DK): 3.5–4.5mm (US sizes 4–7)
Aran or worsted weight: 4.5–5.5mm (US sizes 7–9)

Yarns and colours

When it comes to making your baby blankets or shawls, there is a wealth of yarn types and colours to choose from. They each have different qualities and will present different effects, so it can be useful to think about what you want to achieve before you buy your materials.

Choosing yarns

There are many yarns on the market that are suitable for making baby blankets and shawls. They may be spun from pure wool, acrylic or cotton, or a blend of two or more of these fibres. Pure wool baby yarns are specially treated to be soft, non-scratchy and machine-washable, but many crafters prefer to make baby items from acrylic yarn because it is inexpensive and easy to care for. Cotton yarns are a good choice for babies living in warm climates, because they are cooler in use than both wool and acrylic yarns.

As well as considering fibre composition, weight is an important factor that will affect your yarn choices. Fine yarns take longer to work up into a large item, such as a lacy shawl, than thicker yarns, but they have the advantage of offering a much longer yardage per ball, and making a beautifully light, soft fabric. Medium-weight yarns are fairly quick to work up and will make a warm and cosy baby blanket, but the yardage is less generous. Heavy yarns are quick to work, but may make a blanket that is too solid and bulky compared to one made in a finer yarn weight, and they also have a very short yardage per ball. In addition, a stitch pattern can look entirely different worked in a fine, medium or heavy yarn.

Choosing colours

Colour choice is a very personal thing, and colours combine with each other in different ways, some of which may appear more or less pleasing to the eye. The colours used to crochet and knit the swatches shown in the directory are merely suggestions – feel free to work the patterns in whatever colours you prefer.

Traditional pastel colours are a good, although rather safe, choice for making baby blankets and shawls. As well as the usual pink and blue shades, plus white and cream, you can choose from pastel greens, turquoises, mauves and yellows. Many ranges of baby yarns include stronger colours, such as purple and orange, as well as pretty variegated yarns.

Left: acrylic and acrylic blends; top centre: pure wool; right: cotton and cotton blends.

Changing colours in a block pattern

There are many ways of combining colours, depending on the effect you want to create, and many of the block patterns will look very different worked in other colour combinations. As an example, take a crochet block pattern and change the colours to see how the design can create different effects.

Changing colours in a stitch pattern

Broken stripes is one of the easiest stitch patterns to knit. As well as changing the yarn colours to make it look different, you can also experiment by varying the number of rows worked in each colour. There are more examples of working with stripes on page 13.

Soft pastel shades of buttery yellow, lavender, blue and green are a pretty, though rather safe, colour combination (Lucy's flower, page 42).

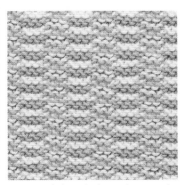

By changing the yarn colours to bright shades of blue, lavender, pink and green, the pattern becomes vibrant and much more lively.

Crisp and clean looking, this swatch is knitted in pale green and white (Broken stripes, page 90).

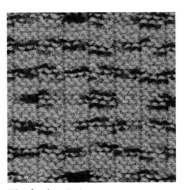

By using two bright colours that are similar in tone, the pattern is shown up much more strongly than when it is knitted in pastels.

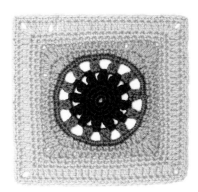

For a different effect, change the yarn to four shades of a single colour and arrange them with the darkest shade at the centre, graduating outwards to the palest shade around the outside of the block.

The final variation uses two colours, one light and one dark. The colours change alternately throughout the block, beginning and ending with the darker colour.

Two shades of the same colour, one light and one dark, make a pleasing contrast on this swatch.

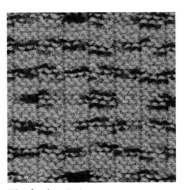

The final variation uses two yarns; the main yarn is solid and the other is variegated. Four rows worked in the main yarn alternate with two rows of the variegated yarn to create a speckled pattern.

Stitch patterns

There are over 80 crochet and knit stitch patterns, in addition to the block patterns. The effects vary from light and lacy filet crochet to make a beautiful layette shawl, right through to colourful intarsia patterns for an everyday buggy blanket. Many of the stitch patterns look fabulous worked in a single colour using a beautifully soft and smooth yarn, but many could also be worked in a variety of textured yarns. Always make a test swatch first. This lets you check the drape of the fabric and the effect of your colours, as well as helping you make sure you like the effect of the finished item.

Filet crochet charts

Choosing a stitch pattern

Choose a stitch pattern that is fairly closely worked to make pram and cot covers, and small blankets for baby to snuggle into. Lighter, lacy patterns are good for making shawls, especially when worked in a fine yarn to avoid large holes that can catch and snag on tiny fingers.

Stitch patterns for blankets

Stitch patterns for shawls

Top left: Grotto, page 74; top right: Cornrows, page 83; bottom left: Leafy rows, page 34; bottom right: Mini checks, page 87.

Top left: Lavender lace, page 88; top right: Alternate shells, page 53; bottom left: Sunday lace, page 82; bottom right: Travelling vines, page 45.

Filet crochet for shawls

Work any of the filet crochet patterns in a fine yarn to make a delightfully lacy shawl or wrap. Repeat the chart to make an all-over pattern, or arrange a row of motifs at each end of a square shawl or rectangular wrap.

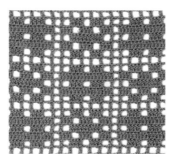

Designed as an all-over pattern, you could also repeat the chart across the ends of a shawl to make a border.

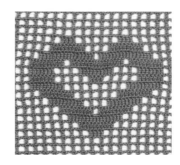

This heart motif would make a pretty border for a rectangular wrap. Work the beginning border from the chart as given, then turn the chart upside down when working the end border so the hearts will face outwards at either end.

Changing effects: striped

It's easy to get a different effect by simply changing the sequence and frequency of the colour changes. For example, take a crochet stitch pattern and see how you can make four different swatches from one pattern.

Changing effects: plain

You can add stripes to many of the solid colour stitch patterns. Take the time to make one or more swatches using your chosen yarns. Below are two stitch patterns, one crochet and one knit, worked in a solid colour and in stripes.

A selection of six boldly contrasting bright colours is arranged in two-row stripes (Interlocking colours, page 20).

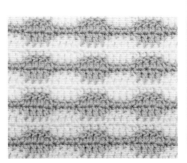

Changing the colours to pale green and cream and limiting the number of colours creates a calmer effect.

This swatch (All yellow, page 40) is worked in a solid colour and shows off the neat, slightly textured pattern.

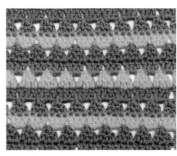

By using three colours arranged in one-row stripes, the effect is different and the stitch looks more exciting.

Try changing the colours to three shades of a single colour and varying the number of rows. Use two rows of the darkest shade, four rows of the medium and six rows of the palest.

The final variation features wide, six-row stripes of the main background colour divided by narrow stripes worked in strongly contrasting colours. Use two colours for each narrow stripe.

This pretty, lacy pattern looks attractive worked in just one colour of yarn (Sunny scallops, page 46).

Introducing a second colour shows off the construction of the stitch pattern and enhances the scallops. Use two rows of the original colour and four rows of the contrast yarn.

Blocks

All the knit and crochet blocks shown in the directory are worked in the same weight of yarn – double knitting (DK) weight – using the same size of needles or hook – 4mm (US size 6) needles, 4mm (US size G) hook. The swatches in the photographs are all the same size – 15cm (6in) square.

You can work the blocks in any weight of yarn you choose, remembering that finer yarn and smaller needle/hook sizes will make the blocks smaller, while heavier yarn and larger needle/hook sizes will make larger blocks. As a general guideline, you can combine any of the crochet blocks shown in the directory with any of the others to make a baby blanket, or combine any of the knitted blocks in one blanket. It's not a good idea, however, to mix crochet and knitted blocks in the same piece as the drape and elasticity of the two techniques is very different.

Choosing blocks

Begin by looking at the blocks in the directory on pages 16–111, and choose several block patterns that appeal to you and are suitable for your current skill level.

Blocks can be smooth, lacy or textured, depending on their technique. They can be worked in straight, diagonal or L-shaped rows, and crochet blocks can also be worked in rounds from the centre outwards. Plain blocks can be decorated with applied motifs to add colour and texture.

Different methods of working

Knitted block worked in straight rows (Textured heart, page 49).

Knitted block worked in diagonal rows (Shades of green, page 56).

Textures and lace

Smooth knitted block (Blue abstract, page 26).

Lacy knitted block (Diagonal lace, page 72).

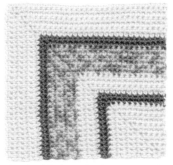

Crochet block worked in L-shaped rows (Turquoise delight, page 22).

Crochet block worked in rounds (Wagon wheel, page 39).

Textured crochet block (Bobble kisses, page 21).

Crochet block with applied motifs (Mallow, page 88).

Creating patterns with blocks

Many of the blocks can be combined in more than one way. When you arrange identical blocks into groups of four or more, and start turning some of the blocks, different patterns start to appear. For example, take a block made from a plain and a striped triangle and see how many patterns you can make.

Planning a design

It is a good idea to make a visual plan before you start combining blocks, so that you can be sure you will be happy with the appearance and size of the finished piece. First, make a swatch of each block you intend to combine, using your chosen yarn colours. The swatches will also serve as gauge/*tension* samples (see page 125) and give you a finished size for your blocks. Mark the outline of the required number of blocks on graph paper, making a grid of squares about 2.5cm (1in) square. Roughly colour the squares with pencils or felt-tip markers in the colours and patterns of the blocks you have chosen.

At the side of the plan, write down the number of blocks you need to make and details of the yarn colours you have selected.

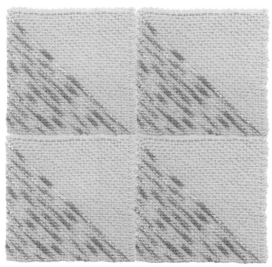

Four blocks placed as shown make a sawtooth pattern that could be repeated across a blanket.

Create a simple diamond shape by combining four blocks so that one colour meets in the centre.

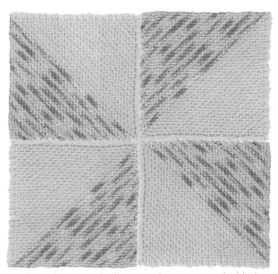

Make a classic windmill pattern by arranging the blocks as shown.

An arrowhead pattern is similar in construction to the diamond, but the bottom blocks are turned upside down.

Block
and
Stitch
Directory

The directory contains photographs
and patterns for 200 blocks, stitch
patterns and edgings worked in
knitting and crochet. Each pattern
is graded by degree of difficulty so
you can choose the ones that suit
your own skill level.

1 Fjord

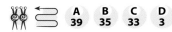

		A	B	C	D
		39	35	33	3

NOTES: Count stitches only after working Row 4. Where possible, don't break yarn at colour changes, instead carry colour not in use loosely up side of work.

Using yarn A, CO a multiple of 3 sts plus 2.

ROW 1: (RS) K1, P1, *YO, K1, YO, P2; rep from * to last 3 sts, YO, K1, YO, P1, K1.

ROW 2: K2, *P3, K2; rep from * to end.

ROW 3: K1, P1, *K3, P2; rep from * to last 5 sts, K3, P1, K1.

ROW 4: K2, *P3tog, K2; rep from * to end.

Rep Rows 1–4, changing yarns in the following colour sequence: 2 rows in yarn A, 2 rows in yarn B, 2 rows in yarn A, 2 rows in yarn B, 2 rows in yarn A, 2 rows in yarn B, 2 rows in yarn C, 2 rows in yarn D, 2 rows in yarn C, 2 rows in yarn D, 2 rows in yarn C, 2 rows in yarn D. Repeat for length required. BO/CO.

2 Bright eyes

			A	B	C	D	E
			37	3	40	5	39

BACKGROUND BLOCK

FOUNDATION CHAIN: Using yarn A, ch 29.

ROW 1: (RS) 1 sc/*dc* into 2nd ch from hook, 1 sc/*dc* into each ch to end, turn. (28 sc/*dc*)

ROW 2: Ch 1, 1 sc/*dc* into each sc/*dc* of previous row, turn.

Rep Row 2 32 times more, ending with a WS row.

Fasten off yarn.

FLOWER MOTIFS (MAKE 4)

FOUNDATION RING: Using yarn B, ch 6 and join with sl st to form a ring.

ROUND 1: Ch 3 (counts as 1 dc/*tr*), 14 dc/*tr* into ring, join with sl st into 3rd of ch-3. Break off yarn B.

ROUND 2: Join yarn C to any dc/*tr*, 1 sc/*dc* into same st, *3 dc/*tr* into each of next 2 dc/*tr*, 1 sc/*dc* into next dc/*tr*; rep from * to last 2 sts, 3 dc/*tr* into each of last 2 dc/*tr*, join with sl st into first sc/*dc*.

Fasten off yarn, leaving a long tail for stitching motif to background. Make one more flower using the same colour combination and two flowers using yarn D instead of yarn B and yarn E instead of yarn C.

After blocking, pin flower motifs to background block using photograph as a guide to placement. Stitch each motif in place with yarn tail, stitching between petals. If the item is to be washed frequently, work more stitches around outside of petals.

Lozenges

  38

CO 32 sts.
Starting at the bottom right-hand corner of the chart, work the 44-row pattern from the chart, reading odd-numbered (RS) rows from right to left and even-numbered (WS) rows from left to right.
BO/CO.

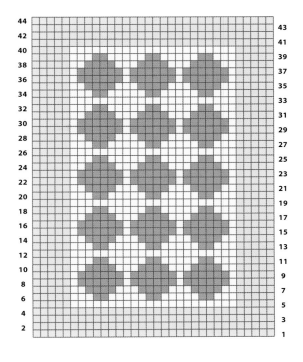

☐ K ON RS ROWS, P ON WS ROWS

☐ K ON BOTH RS AND WS ROWS

■ P ON RS ROWS, K ON WS ROWS

  ## Blue skies

37

FOUNDATION CHAIN: Work a multiple of 6 chains plus 3.
ROW 1: (RS) 1 dc/*tr* into 4th ch from hook, 1 dc/*tr* in each ch to end, turn.
ROW 2: Ch 1, 1 sc/*dc* into first dc/*tr*, *ch 2, sk next 2 dc/*tr*, 1 dc/*tr* into next dc/*tr*, ch 2, sk next 2 dc/*tr*, 1 sc/*dc* into next sc/*dc*; rep from * working last sc/*dc* into 3rd of beg skipped ch-3, turn.

ROW 3: Ch 3, 2 dc/*tr* into first sc/*dc*, *1 sc/*dc* into next dc/*tr*, 5 dc/*tr* into next sc/*dc*; rep from * ending last rep with 3 dc/*tr* into last sc/*dc*, turn.
ROW 4: Ch 1, 1 sc/*dc* into first dc/*tr*, *ch 2, 1 dc/*tr* into next sc/*dc*, ch 2, sk next 2 dc/*tr*, 1 sc/*dc* into next sc/*dc*; rep from * ending last rep with 1 sc/*dc* into 3rd of ch-3, turn.
ROW 5: Ch 3, *2 dc/*tr* into next ch-2

sp, 1 dc/*tr* into next dc/*tr*, 2 dc/*tr* into next ch-2 sp, 1 dc/*tr* into next sc/*dc*; rep from * to end, turn.
ROW 6: Ch 1, 1 sc/*dc* into first dc/*tr*, *ch 2, sk next 2 dc/*tr*, 1 dc/*tr* into next dc/*tr*, ch 2, sk next 2 dc/*tr*, 1 sc/*dc* into next sc/*dc*; rep from * working last sc/*dc* in 3rd of ch-3, turn.
Rep Rows 3–6 for length required.
Fasten off yarn.

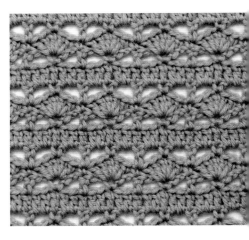

5 Lacy stripes

Using yarn A, CO a multiple of 2 sts plus 1.

ROW 1: (RS) K.

ROWS 2 & 3: Rep Row 1.

ROW 4: K1, *P2tog, YO; rep from * to last 2 sts, P1, K1.

ROWS 5–7: Rep Row 1.

ROW 8: K1, P to last st, K1.

Rep Rows 1–8, changing yarns in the following colour sequence: 8 rows in yarn A, 8 rows in yarn B. Repeat for length required. BO/CO.

6 Interlocking colours

FOUNDATION CHAIN: Using yarn A, work a multiple of 8 chains plus 5.

ROW 1: (RS) 1 sc/*dc* into 2nd ch from hook, 1 sc/*dc* into each of next 3 chs, *1 dc/*tr* into each of next 4 chs, 1 sc/*dc* into each of next 4 chs; rep from * to end, turn.

ROW 2: Ch 1, 1 sc/*dc* into each of next 4 sc/*dc*, *1 dc/*tr* into each of next 4 dc/*tr*, 1 sc/*dc* into each of next 4 sc/*dc*; rep from * to end, turn.

ROW 3: Ch 3 (counts as 1 dc/*tr*), sk first sc/*dc*, 1 dc/*tr* into each of next 3 sc/*dc*, *1 sc/*dc* into each of next 4 dc/*tr*, 1 dc/*tr* into each of next 4 sc/*dc*; rep from * to end, turn.

ROW 4: Ch 3, sk first st, 1 dc/*tr* into each of next 3 dc/*tr*, *1 sc/*dc* into each of next 4 sc/*dc*, 1 dc/*tr* into each of next 4 dc/*tr*; rep from * to end, working last dc/*tr* into 3rd of ch-3, turn.

ROW 5: Ch 1, 1 sc/*dc* into each of next 4 dc/*tr*, *1 dc/*tr* into each of next 4 sc/*dc*, 1 sc/*dc* into each of next 4 dc/*tr*; rep from * to end, working last sc/*dc* into 3rd of ch-3, turn.

Rep Rows 2–5, changing yarns in the following colour sequence: 2 rows in yarn A, 2 rows in yarn B, 2 rows in yarn C, 2 rows in yarn D, 2 rows in yarn E, 2 rows in yarn F. Repeat for length required. Fasten off yarn.

7 Bright & bold

A	B	C	D
21	32	48	52

Using yarn A, CO 31 sts and K 1 row.

ROW 1: (RS) K14, sl 1, K2tog, psso, K14.

ROW 2: K.

ROW 3: K13, sl 1, K2tog, psso, K13.

ROW 4: K.

Cont working in this way, dec 2 sts at the centre of every RS (odd-numbered) row until 3 sts remain on the needle, ending with a WS row.

NEXT ROW: K3tog.

Fasten off yarn.

Make three more blocks using yarns B, C and D. Using the photograph as a guide to position, join the cast-on edges of the four blocks together using the overcasting method of joining shown on page 116.

8 Bobble kisses

21

SPECIAL ABBREVIATION:

MB = make bobble (keeping last loop of each stitch on hook, work 5 dc/*tr* into same stitch, YO and draw yarn through all 6 loops).

FOUNDATION CHAIN: Ch 30.

ROW 1: (RS) 1 sc/*dc* into 2nd ch from hook, 1 sc/*dc* into each ch to end, turn. (29 dc/*tr*)

ROW 2: Ch 1, 1 sc/*dc* into each sc/*dc* to end, turn.

ROWS 3–5: Rep Row 2.

ROW 6: Ch 1, 1 sc/*dc* into each of next 3 sc/*dc*, *MB, 1 sc/*dc* into each of next 7 sc/*dc*, MB, **1 sc/*dc* into each of next 5 sc/*dc*; rep from * to ** once more, 1 sc/*dc* into each of next 3 sc/*dc*, turn.

ROW 7 AND EVERY ALT ROW: Rep Row 2.

ROW 8: Ch 1, 1 sc/*dc* into each of next 5 sc/*dc*, *MB, 1 sc/*dc* into each of next 3 sc/*dc*, MB, **1 sc/*dc* into each of next 9 sc/*dc*; rep from * to ** once more, 1 sc/*dc* into each of next 5 sc/*dc*, turn.

ROW 10: Ch 1, 1 sc/*dc* into each of next 7 sc/*dc*, MB, 1 sc/*dc* into each of next 13 sc/*dc*, MB, 1 sc/*dc* into each of next 7 sc/*dc*, turn.

ROW 12: Rep Row 8.

ROW 14: Rep Row 6.

ROWS 16 & 18: Rep Row 2.

ROWS 20, 22, 24, 26 & 28: Rep Rows 6, 8, 10, 8 & 6.

ROWS 29–32: Rep Row 2.

ROW 33: Ch 1, 1 sc/*dc* into each sc/*dc* to end, turn. Fasten off yarn.

9 Turquoise delight

A	B	C
26	46	47

FOUNDATION CHAIN: Using yarn A, ch 2.

ROW 1: (RS) 3 sc/*dc* into 2nd ch from hook, turn. (3 sc/*dc*)

ROW 2: Ch 1, 1 sc/*dc* into first sc/*dc*, 3 sc/*dc* into next sc/*dc*, 1 sc/*dc* into last sc/*dc*, turn. (5 sc/*dc*)

ROW 3: Ch 1, 1 sc/*dc* into each of next 2 sc/*dc*, 3 sc/*dc* into next sc/*dc*,

1 sc/*dc* into each of next 2 sc/*dc*, turn. (7 sc/*dc*)

ROW 4: Ch 1, 1 sc/*dc* into each of next 3 sc/*dc*, 3 sc/*dc* into next sc/*dc*, 1 sc/*dc* into each of next 3 sc/*dc*, turn. (9 sc/*dc*)

Cont to increase as set, working 3 sc/*dc* into the centre stitch of every row, changing colours in

the following sequence and ending with a RS row: 10 rows in yarn A, 2 rows in yarn B, 4 rows in yarn A, 6 rows in yarn C, 2 rows in yarn B, 7 rows in yarn A. Fasten off yarn.

10 All-over crosses

 69

REPEAT SIZE: 12 blocks high by 12 blocks wide.

NOTE: The two cross motifs repeat across the mesh background. Alternatively, scatter individual motifs at random across the mesh background.

WORKING THE REPEAT PATTERN: Begin working the pattern from the chart, repeating the section of the chart inside the blue lines. Starting at the bottom right-hand corner of the chart, work the blocks and spaces from the chart in filet

crochet (see page 121). When following the chart, read odd-numbered (RS) rows from right to left and even-numbered (WS) rows from left to right. Fasten off yarn.

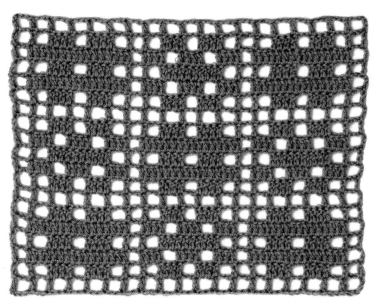

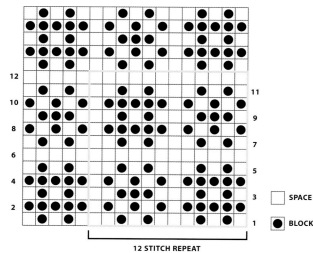

☐ SPACE
● BLOCK

12 STITCH REPEAT

11 Shell lattice

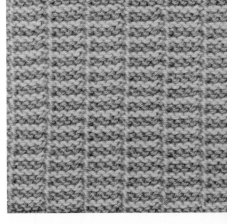

111 ⇄ **45**

FOUNDATION CHAIN: Work a multiple of 10 chains plus 3.
ROW 1: (RS) 1 dc/*tr* into 4th ch from hook, 1 dc/*tr* into next ch, *sk next 2 chs, [1 dc/*tr*, ch 3, 1 dc/*tr*] into next ch, sk next 2 chs, 1 dc/*tr* into each of next 5 chs; rep from * ending last rep with 1 dc/*tr* into each of last 3 chs, turn.
ROW 2: Ch 3, sk first 2 dc/*tr*, 1 dc/*tr* into next dc/*tr*, ch 2, 5 dc/*tr* into next ch-3 sp, *ch 2, dc2tog/*tr2tog* into first and 5th sts of next 5 dc/*tr* group, ch 2, 5 dc/*tr* into next ch-3 sp; rep from * ending with ch 2, dc2tog/*tr2tog* over next dc/*tr* and 3rd of beg skipped ch-3, turn.

ROW 3: Ch 4, 1 dc/*tr* into inverted V made by first dc2tog/*tr2tog*, *1 dc/*tr* into each of next 5 dc/*tr*, [1 dc/*tr*, ch 3, 1 dc/*tr*] into inverted V made by next dc2tog/*tr2tog*; rep from * ending last rep with [1 dc/*tr*, ch 1, 1 dc/*tr*] into sp made by turning ch of previous row, turn.
ROW 4: Ch 3, 2 dc/*tr* into ch-1 sp, *ch 2, dc2tog/*tr2tog* into first and 5th sts of next 5 dc/*tr* group, ch 2, 5 dc/*tr* into next ch-3 sp; rep from * ending last rep with 3 dc/*tr* into sp made by turning ch, turn.
ROW 5: Ch 3, sk first dc/*tr*, 1 dc/*tr* into each of next 2 dc/*tr*, *[1 dc/*tr*,

ch 3, 1 dc/*tr*] into inverted V made by next dc2tog/*tr2tog*, 1 dc/*tr* into each of next 5 dc/*tr*; rep from * ending last rep with 1 dc/*tr* into each of last 2 dc/*tr*, 1 dc/*tr* into 3rd of ch-3, turn.
ROW 6: Ch 3, sk first 2 dc/*tr*, 1 dc/*tr* into next dc/*tr*, ch 2, 5 dc/*tr* into next ch-3 sp, *ch 2, dc2tog/*tr2tog* into first and 5th sts of next 5 dc/*tr* group, ch 2, 5 dc/*tr* into next ch-3 sp; rep from * ending with ch 2, dc2tog/*tr2tog* over next dc/*tr* and 3rd of ch-3, turn.
Rep Rows 3–6 for length required. Fasten off yarn.

12 Slipped stripes

 ⇄ **A 4** **B 45**

NOTES: Slip all stitches purlwise keeping yarn on wrong side of work. Don't break yarn at colour changes, instead carry colour not in use loosely up side of work.

Using yarn A, CO a multiple of 5 sts plus 3.
ROW 1: (RS) K1, *sl 1, K4; rep from * to last 2 sts, sl 1, K1.
ROW 2: K.
Rep Rows 1 & 2, changing yarns in the following colour sequence:
2 rows in yarn A, 2 rows in yarn B.
Repeat for length required.
BO/*CO*.

13 Chevron lace

16

CO 31 sts and K 2 rows.

ROW 1: (RS) K2, *K4, YO, sl 1, K1, psso, K3; rep from * to last 2 sts, K2.

ROW 2 AND EVERY ALT ROW: K2, P to last 2 sts, K2.

ROW 3: K2, *K2, K2tog, YO, K1, YO, sl 1, K1, psso, K2; rep from * to last 2 sts, K2.

ROW 5: K2, *K1, K2tog, YO, K3, YO, sl 1, K1, psso, K1; rep from * to last 2 sts, K2.

ROW 7: K2, *K2tog, YO, K5, YO, sl 1, K1, psso; rep from * to last 2 sts, K2.

ROW 8: K2, P to last 2 sts. Rep Rows 1–8 three times more, ending with a Row 8. Rep Rows 1–7 once more. K 2 rows. BO/CO.

14 Pink heart

17

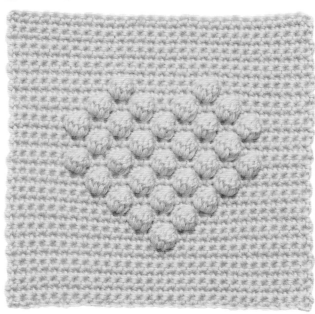

SPECIAL ABBREVIATION:

MB = make bobble (keeping last loop of each stitch on hook, work 5 dc/tr into same stitch, YO and draw yarn through all 6 loops).

FOUNDATION CHAIN: Ch 30.

ROW 1: (WS) 1 sc/dc into 2nd ch from hook, 1 sc/dc into each ch to end, turn. (29 sc/dc)

ROW 2: Ch 1, 1 sc/dc into each sc/dc to end, turn.

ROWS 3–8: Rep Row 2.

ROW 9: Ch 1, 1 sc/dc into each of next 14 sc/dc, MB, 1 sc/dc into each of next 14 sc/dc, turn.

ROW 10 AND EVERY ALT ROW: Rep Row 2.

ROW 11: Ch 1, 1 sc/dc into each of next 12 sc/dc, MB, 1 sc/dc into each of next 3 sc/dc, MB, 1 sc/dc into each of next 12 sc/dc, turn.

ROW 13: Ch 1, 1 sc/dc into each of next 10 sc/dc, [MB, 1 sc/dc in each of next 3 sc/dc] twice, MB, 1 sc/dc in each of next 10 sc/dc, turn.

ROWS 15, 19 & 23: Ch 1, 1 sc/dc into each of next 8 sc/dc, [MB, 1 sc/dc into each of next 3 sc/dc] three times, MB, 1 sc/dc into each of next 8 sc/dc, turn.

ROWS 17 & 21: Ch 1, 1 sc/dc into each of next 6 sc/dc, [MB, 1 sc/dc into each of next 3 sc/dc] four times, MB, 1 sc/dc into each of next 6 sc/dc, turn.

ROW 25: Ch 1, 1 sc/dc into each of next 10 sc/dc, MB, 1 sc/dc into each of next 7 sc/dc, MB, 1 sc/dc into each of next 10 sc/dc, turn.

ROWS 26–32: Rep Row 1.

ROW 33: Ch 1, 1 sc/dc into each sc/dc to end, turn. Fasten off yarn.

15 Shell stripes

FOUNDATION CHAIN: Using yarn A, work a multiple of 6 chains plus 2.

ROW 1: (WS) 1 sc/*dc* into 2nd ch from hook, 1 sc/*dc* into next ch, *ch 3, sk next 3 chs, 1 sc/*dc* into each of next 3 ch; rep from * to last 5 chs, ch 3, sk next 3 chs, 1 sc/*dc* into each of last 2 chs, turn.

ROW 2: Ch 1, 1 sc/*dc* into first sc/*dc*, *5 dc/*tr* into ch-3 sp, sk 1 sc/*dc*, 1 sc/*dc* into next sc/*dc*; rep from * to end, turn.

ROW 3: Ch 3, *1 sc/*dc* into 2nd, 3rd and 4th stitches of 5 dc/*tr* group, ch 3; rep from * to end, ending with 1 sc/*dc* into 2nd, 3rd and 4th stitches of 5 dc/*tr* group, ch 2, 1 sc/*dc* into last st, turn.

ROW 4: Ch 3, 2 dc/*tr* into ch-2 sp, sk 1 sc/*dc*, 1 sc/*dc* into next sc/*dc*,
*5 dc/*tr* into ch-3 sp, sk 1 sc/*dc*, 1 sc/*dc* into next sc/*dc*; rep from * to end, 3 dc/*tr* into last ch-3 sp, turn.

ROW 5: Ch 1, 1 sc/*dc* into each of first 2 dc/*tr*, *ch 3, 1 sc/*dc* into 2nd, 3rd and 4th stitches of 5 dc/*tr* group; rep from * to end, ending with ch 3, 1 sc/*dc* into 2nd dc/*tr*, 1 sc/*dc* into 3rd of ch-3, turn.
Rep Rows 2–5, changing yarns in the following colour sequence: 5 rows in yarn A, *2 rows in yarn B, 4 rows in yarn C, 2 rows in yarn B, 4 rows in yarn A. Repeat from * for length required. Fasten off yarn.

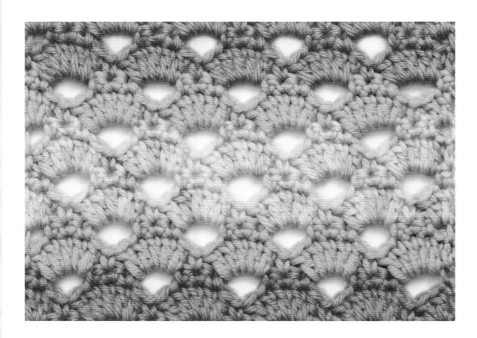

16 Stripes & lace

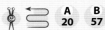

NOTE: At colour changes, do not break yarn, but carry colour not in use up side of work.

Using yarn A, CO a multiple of 2 sts plus 1.

ROW 1: (RS) K.

ROWS 2 & 3: Rep Row 1.

ROW 4: K1, *P2tog, YO; rep from * to last 2 sts, P1, K1.

ROWS 5, 7, 9 & 11: Rep Row 1.

ROWS 6, 8, 10 & 12: K1, P to last st, K1.
Rep Rows 1–12, changing yarns in the following colour sequence: 6 rows in yarn A, 2 rows in yarn B, 2 rows in yarn A, 2 rows in yarn B. Repeat for length required. BO/*CO*.

17 Bobble blocks

SPECIAL ABBREVIATION:
MB = make bobble (keeping last loop of each stitch on hook, work 5 dc/*tr* into same stitch, YO and draw yarn through all 6 loops).

FOUNDATION CHAIN: Ch 30.
ROW 1: (RS) 1 sc/*dc* into 2nd ch from hook, 1 sc/*dc* into each ch to end, turn. (29 dc/*tr*)
ROW 2: Ch 1, 1 sc/*dc* into each sc/*dc* to end, turn.
ROWS 3–5: Rep Row 2.
ROWS 6, 8, 10 & 12: Ch 1, 1 sc/*dc* into each of next 3 sc/*dc*, *[MB, 1 sc/*dc* into next sc/*dc*] four times, 1 sc/*dc* into each of next 8 sc/*dc*; rep from * once more, 1 sc/*dc* into each of next 2 sc/*dc*, turn.

ROW 7 AND EVERY ALT ROW: Rep Row 2.
ROWS 14, 16, 18 & 20: Ch 1, 1 sc/*dc* into each of next 11 sc/*dc*, [MB, 1 sc/*dc* into next sc/*dc*] four times, 1 sc/*dc* into each of next 10 sc/*dc*, turn.
ROWS 20, 22, 24 & 26: Rep Row 6.
ROWS 29–32: Rep Row 2.
ROW 33: Ch 1, 1 sc/*dc* into each sc/*dc* to end, turn.
Fasten off yarn.

18 Blue abstract

Using yarn A, CO 33 sts. Starting at the bottom right-hand corner of the chart, work the 42-row pattern from the chart, reading odd-numbered (RS) rows (K all sts) from right to left and even-numbered (WS) rows (P all sts) from left to right. BO/*CO*.

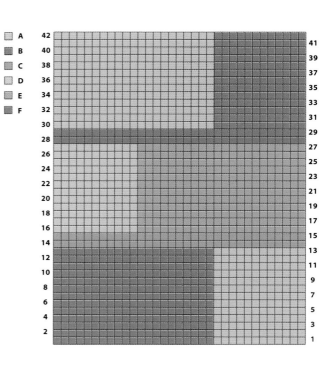

19 Christopher's stripes

| A 24 | B 40 | C 50 |

NOTE: Don't break main yarn at colour changes, instead carry it loosely up side of work.

Using yarn A, CO a multiple of 2 sts plus 1.

ROW 1: (WS) K1, P to last st, K1.

ROW 2: K1, *P1, K1; rep from * to end.

Rep Rows 1 & 2, changing yarns in the following colour sequence: 6 rows in yarn A, 2 rows in yarn B, 2 rows in yarn A, 2 rows in yarn C.
Repeat for length required.
BO/*CO*.

20 Baby blue

 40

FOUNDATION CHAIN: Work a multiple of 3 chains plus 2.

ROW 1: (WS) 1 sc/*dc* into 2nd ch from hook, *ch 3, sk next 2 chs, 1 sc/*dc* into next sc/*dc*; rep from * to end, turn.

ROW 2: Ch 3, 1 dc/*tr* into first sc/*dc*, *1 sc/*dc* into next ch-3 sp, 3 dc/*tr* into next sc/*dc*; rep from * ending last rep with 2 dc/*tr* into last sc/*dc*, turn.

ROW 3: Ch 1, 1 sc/*dc* into first sc/*dc*, *ch 3, 1 sc/*dc* into centre st of next 3 dc/*tr* group; rep from * working last sc/*dc* into 3rd of ch-3, turn.
Rep Rows 2 & 3 for length required.
Fasten off yarn.

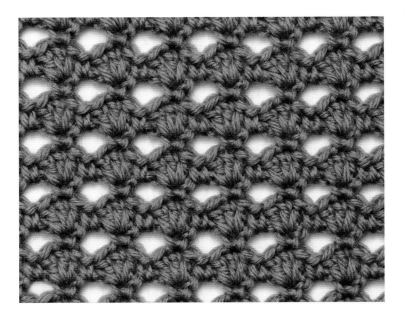

21 Creamy waves

 **A 2** **B 3**

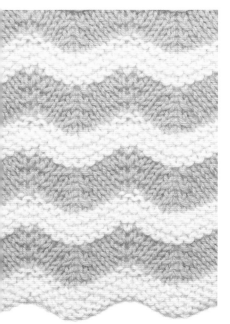

SPECIAL ABBREVIATION:

INC = increase by knitting into front and back of indicated stitch.

Using yarn A, CO a multiple of 11 sts.
ROW 1: (WS) K.
ROWS 2–5: Rep Row 1.
ROW 6: *K2tog, K2, [inc into next st] twice, K3, sl 1, K1, psso; rep from * to end.
ROW 7: K1, P to last st, K1.
ROWS 8 & 10: Rep Row 6.
ROWS 9 & 11: Rep Row 7.
ROW 12: K.
Rep Rows 1–12, changing yarns in the following colour sequence: 5 rows in yarn A, *6 rows in yarn B, 6 rows in yarn A. Rep from * for length required. BO/CO.

23 Dash

 **A 57** **B 8**

FOUNDATION CHAIN: Using yarn A, ch 29.
ROW 1: (RS) 1 sc/*dc* into 2nd ch from hook, 1 sc/*dc* into each ch to end, turn. (28 sc/*dc*)
ROW 2: Ch 1, 1 sc/*dc* into each sc/*dc* of previous row, turn.
Rep Row 2 32 more times, ending with a WS row.
Fasten off yarn.
Using lengths of yarn B threaded in a yarn needle, work parallel rows of evenly spaced running stitches horizontally across the block.

22 Warm zigzags

 A 8 **B 6** **C 58** **D 2**

FOUNDATION CHAIN: Using yarn A, work a multiple of 11 chains plus 2.
ROW 1: (RS) 2 sc/*dc* into 2nd ch from hook, *1 sc/*dc* into each of next 4 chs, sk next 2 chs, 1 sc/*dc* into each of next 4 chs, 3 sc/*dc* into next ch; rep from * to end, ending last rep with 2 sc/*dc* into last ch, turn.
ROW 2: Ch 1, 2 sc/*dc* into first sc/*dc*, *1 sc/*dc* into each of next 4 sc/*dc*, sk next 2 sc/*dc*, 1 sc/*dc* into each of next 4 sc/*dc*, 3 sc/*dc* into next sc/*dc*;

rep from * to end, ending last rep with 2 sc/*dc* into last sc/*dc*, turn.
Rep Row 2, changing yarns in the following colour sequence: 2 rows in yarn A, 2 rows in yarn B, 2 rows in yarn C, 2 rows in yarn D.
Repeat for length required.
Fasten off yarn.

24 Amber leaf

SPECIAL ABBREVIATION:

INC = increase by knitting into front and back of first stitch.

Using yarn A, CO 3 sts.
ROW 1: (RS) Inc, K2.
ROW 2: Inc, K3.
ROW 3: Inc, K1, YO, K1, YO, K2.
ROW 4: Inc, K1, P3, K3.
ROW 5: Inc, K3, YO, K1, YO, K4.
ROW 6: Inc, K2, P5, K4.
ROW 7: Inc, K5, YO, K1, YO, K6.
ROW 8: Inc, K3, P7, K5.
ROW 9: Inc, K7, YO, K1, YO, K8.
ROW 10: Inc, K4, P9, K6.
ROW 11: Inc, K9, YO, K1, YO, K10.
ROW 12: Inc, K5, P11, K7.
ROW 13: Inc, K11, YO, K1, YO, K12.
ROW 14: Inc, K6, P13, K8.
ROW 15: Inc, K13, YO, K1, YO, K14.
ROW 16: Inc, K7, P15, K9.
ROW 17: Inc, K8, sl 1, K1, psso, K11, K2tog, K9.
ROW 18: Inc, K8, P13, K10.
ROW 19: Inc, K9, sl 1, K1, psso, K9, K2tog, K10.

ROW 20: Inc, K9, P11, K11.
ROW 21: Inc, K10, sl 1, K1, psso, K7, K2tog, K11.
ROW 22: Inc, K10, P9, K12.
ROW 23: Inc, K11, sl 1, K1, psso, K5, K2tog, K12.
ROW 24: Inc, K11, P7, K13.
ROW 25: Inc, K12, sl 1, K1, psso, K3, K2tog, K13.
ROW 26: Inc, K12, P5, K14.
ROW 27: Inc, K13, sl 1, K1, psso, K1, K2tog, K14.
ROW 28: Inc, K13, P3, K15.
ROW 29: Inc, K14, sl 1, K2tog, psso, K15.
ROWS 30–33: Inc, K to end.
ROWS 34 & 37: Inc, P to last st, K1.
ROWS 35 & 36: Inc, K to end.
ROW 38: Inc, K to end.
ROWS 39, 41 & 42: K2tog, K to end.
ROWS 40 & 43: K2tog, P to last st, K1.
ROW 44: K2tog, K to end.
Rep Rows 39–44 until 4 sts rem on needle, ending with a RS row.
NEXT ROW: K2tog twice.
NEXT ROW: K2tog.
Fasten off yarn.

25 Candyfloss

FOUNDATION CHAIN: Work a multiple of 6 chains plus 2.

ROW 1: (RS) 1 sc/*dc* into 2nd ch from hook, *sk next 2 chs, 7 dc/*tr* into next ch, sk next 2 chs, 1 sc/*dc* into next ch; rep from * to end, turn.

ROW 2: Ch 4 (counts as 1 tr/*dtr*), sk first dc/*tr*, 1 dc/*tr* into each of next 5 dc/*tr*, *sk next dc/*tr*, next sc/*dc* and next dc/*tr*, 1 dc/*tr* into each of next 5 dc/*tr*; rep from * ending with sk last dc/*tr*, 1 tr/*dtr* into sc/*dc*, turn.

ROW 3: Ch 3 (counts as 1 dc/*tr*), 3 dc/*tr* into first tr/*dtr*, *1 sc/*dc* into centre st of next 5 dc/*tr* group, 7 dc/*tr* into next sp between two 5 dc/*tr* groups; rep from * ending

with 4 dc/*tr* into 4th of ch-4, turn.

ROW 4: Ch 3, sk first dc/*tr*, 1 dc/*tr* into each of next 2 dc/*tr*, *sk next dc/*tr*, next sc/*dc* and next dc/*tr*, 1 dc/*tr* into each of next 5 dc/*tr*; rep from * ending with 1 dc/*tr* into each of last 2 dc/*tr*, 1 dc/*tr* into 3rd of ch-3, turn.

ROW 5: Ch 1, 1 sc/*dc* into first dc/*tr*, 7 dc/*tr* into sp between 3 dc/*tr* group and first 5 dc/*tr* group, *1 sc/*dc* into centre st of next 5 dc/*tr* group, 7 dc/*tr* into next sp between two 5 dc/*tr* groups; rep from * ending with 1 sc/*dc* into 3rd of ch-3, turn.

Rep Rows 2–5 for length required. Fasten off yarn.

26 Hot stripes

 | A 22 | B 14 | C 39 | D 13 | E 15 | F 28 |

NOTE: Don't break main yarn at colour changes, instead carry it loosely up side of work.

Using yarn A, CO 33 sts.

ROW 1: (RS) *K1, P1; rep from * to last st, K1.

ROWS 2, 3 & 4: Rep Row 1.

ROW 5: Using yarn B, [K1, P1] twice, K25, [P1, K1] twice.

ROW 6: Using yarn B, [K1, P1] twice, P25, [P1, K1] twice.

Rep Rows 5 & 6 16 times more, ending with a Row 6, at the same time change colours in the following sequence:
2 rows in yarn A, 2 rows in yarn C, 2 rows in yarn A, 2 rows in yarn D, 2 rows in yarn A, 2 rows in yarn E, 2 rows in

yarn A, 2 rows in yarn F, 2 rows in yarn A, 2 rows in yarn E, 2 rows in yarn A, 2 rows in yarn D, 2 rows in yarn A,

2 rows in yarn C, 2 rows in yarn A, 2 rows in yarn B.
Using yarn A, rep Rows 1–4 once more. BO/*CO*.

27 Pin spots

 | A 39 | B 14 | C 22 | D 13 |

NOTES: Slip all stitches purlwise keeping yarn on wrong side of work. Don't break main yarn at colour changes, instead carry it loosely up side of work.

Using yarn A, CO a multiple of 2 sts plus 1.

ROW 1: (RS) K.

ROWS 2, 3 & 4: Rep Row 1.

ROWS 5 & 6: K1, *sl 1, K1.

Rep Rows 1–6, changing yarns in the following colour sequence:
4 rows in yarn A, 2 rows in yarn B, 4 rows in yarn A, 2 rows in yarn C, 4 rows in yarn A, 2 rows in yarn D.
Repeat for length required. BO/*CO*.

28 Warm red

A 15 · B 14 · C 13

FOUNDATION RING: Using yarn A, ch 6 and join with sl st to form a ring.

ROUND 1: Ch 3 (counts as 1 dc/*tr*), 2 dc/*tr* into ring, ch 3, *3 dc/*tr* into ring, ch 3; rep from * twice more, join with sl st into 3rd of ch-3.

ROUND 2: Sl st into each of next 2 dc/*tr* and into next ch-3 sp, ch 3, [2 dc/*tr*, ch 3, 3 dc/*tr*] into same sp, *ch 1, [3 dc/*tr*, ch 3, 3 dc/*tr*] into next ch-3 sp; rep from * twice more, join with sl st into 3rd of ch-3.

ROUND 3: Ch 1, 1 sc/*dc* into same sp, 1 sc/*dc* into each dc/*tr* and ch-1 sp of previous round, working 5 sc/*dc* into each ch-3 corner sp, join with sl st into first sc/*dc*. Break off yarn A.

ROUND 4: Join yarn B. Ch 3, 1 dc/*tr* into each of next 4 sc/*dc*, *[2 dc/*tr*, ch 2, 2 dc/*tr*] into next sc/*dc*, **1 dc/*tr* into each of next 11 sc/*dc*; rep from * twice and from * to ** once more, 1 dc/*tr* into each of next 6 sc/*dc*, join with sl st into 3rd of ch-3.

ROUND 5: Ch 3, 1 dc/*tr* into each of next 6 dc/*tr*, [2 dc/*tr*, ch 2, 2 dc/*tr*] into next ch-2 sp, *1 dc/*tr* into each of next 15 sc/*dc*, [2 dc/*tr*, ch 2, 2 dc/*tr*] into next ch-2 sp; rep from * twice more, 1 dc/*tr* into each of next 8 sc/*dc*, join with sl st into 3rd of ch-3. Break off yarn B.

ROUND 6: Join yarn C to any ch-3 sp, ch 4 (counts as 1 dc/*tr*, ch 1), [1 dc/*tr*, ch 1, 1 dc/*tr*] into same ch-3 sp, *[ch 1, sk next dc/*tr*, 1 dc/*tr* into next dc/*tr*] nine times, ch 1, **[1 dc/*tr*, ch 1, 1 dc/*tr*, ch 1, 1 dc/*tr*] into next ch-3 sp; rep from * twice and from * to ** once more, ch 1, join with sl st into 3rd of ch-4.

ROUND 7: Ch 4, *[1 dc/*tr*, ch 1, 1 dc/*tr*, ch 1, 1 dc/*tr*] into next dc/*tr*, **[ch 1, 1 dc/*tr* into next dc/*tr*] 11 times, ch 1; rep from * twice and from * to ** once more, [ch 1, 1 dc/*tr* into next dc/*tr*] ten times, ch 1, join with sl st into 3rd of ch-3.

ROUND 8: Ch 1, 1 sc/*dc* into same place, 1 sc/*dc* into each dc/*tr* and ch-1 sp of previous round, working 2 sc/*dc* into centre dc/*tr* of each corner group, join with sl st into first sc/*dc*. Fasten off yarn.

29 All-over dots

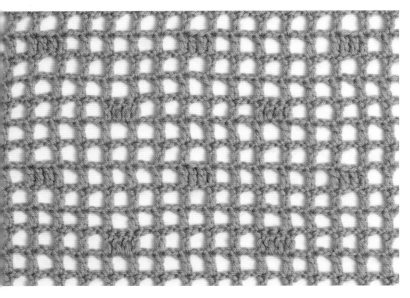

REPEAT SIZE: 6 blocks high by 6 blocks wide.

NOTE: The dot pattern repeats across the mesh background.

WORKING THE REPEAT PATTERN: Begin working the pattern from the chart, repeating the section of the chart inside the green lines. Starting at the bottom right-hand corner of the chart, work the blocks and spaces from the chart in filet crochet (see page 121). When following the chart, read odd-numbered (RS) rows from right to left and even-numbered (WS) rows from left to right. Fasten off yarn.

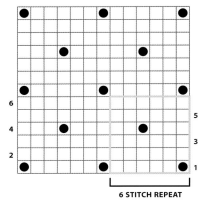

6 STITCH REPEAT

☐ SPACE

● BLOCK

30 Checks

A	B	C	D
50	55	53	5

Using yarn A, CO 33 sts. Starting at the bottom right-hand corner of the chart, work the 42-row pattern from the chart, reading odd-numbered (RS) rows (K all sts) from right to left and even-numbered (WS) rows (P all sts) from left to right. BO/CO.

☐ A
☐ B
☐ C
☐ D

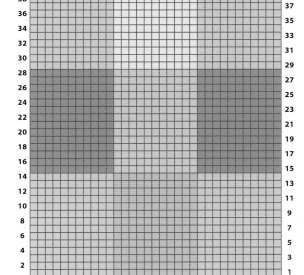

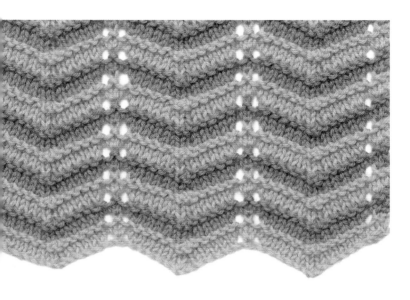

31 Country ripples

   A 52   B 56

NOTE: At colour changes, don't break main yarn, instead carry it loosely up side of work.

Using yarn A, CO a multiple of 14 sts plus 3.
ROW 1: (RS) K2, *YO, K5, K3tog, K5, YO, K1; rep from * to last st, K1.
ROW 2: K1, P to last st, K1.
ROW 3: K.
ROW 4: K.

Rep Rows 1–4, changing yarns in the following colour sequence:
4 rows in yarn A, 4 rows in yarn B.
Repeat for length required.
BO/CO.

32 Patrick's lace

 53

NOTE: Either side can be used as RS.

FOUNDATION CHAIN: Work a multiple of 10 chains plus 7.
ROW 1: 1 dc/tr into 4th ch from hook, 1 dc/tr into each of next 3 chs, *ch 5, sk next 2 chs, 1 sc/dc into next ch, ch 5, sk next 2 chs, 1 dc/tr into each of next 5 chs; rep from * to end, turn.
ROW 2: Ch 3 (counts as 1 dc/tr), sk first dc/tr, 1 dc/tr into each of next 4 dc/tr, *ch 3, 1 sc/dc into next ch-5 sp, ch 3, 1 sc/dc into next ch-5 sp, ch 3, 1 dc/tr into each of next 5 dc/tr; rep from * working last dc/tr into 3rd of beg skipped ch-3, turn.
ROW 3: Ch 3, sk first dc/tr, 1 dc/tr into each of next 4 dc/tr, *sk next ch-3 sp, 7 dc/tr into next ch-3 sp, 1 dc/tr into each of next 5 dc/tr;

rep from * working last dc/tr into 3rd of ch-3, turn.
ROW 4: Ch 3, sk first dc/tr, 1 dc/tr into each of next 4 dc/tr, *ch 5, sk next 3 dc/tr, 1 sc/dc into next dc/tr, ch 5, sk next 3 dc/tr, 1 dc/tr into each of next 5 dc/tr; rep from * working last dc/tr into 3rd of ch-3, turn.
ROW 5: Ch 3, sk first dc/tr, 1 dc/tr into each of next 4 dc/tr, *ch 3, 1 sc/dc into next ch-5 sp, ch 3, 1 sc/dc into next ch-5 sp, ch 3, 1 dc/tr into each of next 5 dc/tr; rep from * working last dc/tr into 3rd of ch-3, turn.
Rep Rows 3–5 for length required.
Fasten off yarn.

33 Leafy rows

  53

CO a multiple of 7 sts plus 1.
ROW 1: (WS) K.
ROWS 2 & 4: K1, P to last st, K1.
ROWS 3 & 5: K.
ROW 6: K1, P6, *YO, K1, YO, P6; rep from * to last st, K1.
ROW 7: K7, *P3, K6; rep from * to last st, K1.
ROW 8: K1, P6, *[K1, YO] twice, K1, P6; rep from * to last st, K1.
ROW 9: K7, *P5, K6; rep from * to last st, K1.
ROW 10: K1, P6, K2, YO, K1, YO, K2, P6; rep from * to last st, K1.
ROW 11: K7, *P7, K6; rep from * to last st, K1.
ROW 12: K1, P6, *K3, YO, K1, YO, K3, P6; rep from * to last st, K1.
ROW 13: K7, *P9, K6; rep from * to last st, K1.

ROW 14: K1, P6, *sl 1, K1, psso, K5, K2tog, P6; rep from * to last st, K1.
ROW 15: K7, *P7, K6; rep from * to last st, K1.
ROW 16: K1, P6, *sl 1, K1, psso, K3, K2tog, P6; rep from * to last st, K1.
ROW 17: K7, *P5, K6; rep from * to last st, K1.
ROW 18: K1, P6, *sl 1, K1, psso, K1, K2tog, P6; rep from * to last st, K1.
ROW 19: K7, *P3, K6; rep from * to last st, K1.
ROW 20: K1, P6, *sl 1, K2tog, psso, P6; rep from * to last st, K1.
Rep Rows 1–20 for length required.
BO/CO.

34 Light & shade

    A 5 B 47

SPECIAL ABBREVIATION:

INC = increase by knitting into front and back of indicated stitch.
NOTE: At colour changes, do not break yarn, but carry colour not in use up side of work.

Using yarn A, CO 1 st and inc in this st. (2 sts)
Beg increase pattern.
ROW 1: (RS) K1, inc in last st.
ROW 2: K2, inc in last st.
Join yarn B.
ROW 3: Using yarn B, K to last st, inc in last st.

Rep Row 3 until there are 43 sts on needle, ending with a RS row. At the same time, change yarn colours every two rows and work alternate two-row stripes of each colour.
K 1 row without shaping.
Break off yarn B.
Beg decrease pattern, using yarn A throughout.
ROW 43: K to last 2 sts, K2tog tbl.
Rep Row 43 until 2 sts rem on needle, ending with a RS row.
NEXT ROW: K2tog tbl.
Fasten off yarn.

35 Baby blocks

 46

FOUNDATION CHAIN: Work a multiple of 5 chains plus 4.
ROW 1: (RS) 1 dc/*tr* into 4th ch from hook, 1 dc/*tr* into each chain to end, turn.
ROW 2: Ch 1, 1 sc/*dc* into each of first 2 dc/*tr*, *ch 3, sk next 3 dc/*tr*, 1 sc/*dc* into each of next 2 dc/*tr*; rep from * working last sc/*dc* into 3rd of beg skipped ch-3, turn.
ROW 3: Ch 3 (counts as 1 dc/*tr*), *5 dc/*tr* into next ch-3 sp; rep from * ending with 1 dc/*tr* into last sc/*dc*, turn.
ROW 4: Ch 1, 1 sc/*dc* into each of first 2 dc/*tr*, *ch 3, sk next 3 dc/*tr*, 1 sc/*dc* into each of next 2 dc/*tr*; rep from * working last sc/*dc* into 3rd of ch-3, turn.
Rep Rows 3 & 4 for length required.
Fasten off yarn.

36 Granny square

A 6   B 32   C 7   D 53   E 5   F 46

FOUNDATION RING: Using yarn A, ch 6 and join with sl st to form a ring.

ROUND 1: Ch 3 (counts as 1 dc/*tr*), 2 dc/*tr* into ring, ch 3, *3 dc/*tr* into ring, ch 3; rep from * twice more, join with sl st into 3rd of ch-3. Break off yarn A.

ROUND 2: Join yarn B to any ch-3 sp, ch 3, [2 dc/*tr*, ch 3, 3 dc/*tr*] into same sp (corner made), *ch 1, [3 dc/*tr*, ch 3, 3 dc/*tr*] into next ch-3 sp; rep from * twice more, ch 1, join with sl st into 3rd of ch-3. Break off yarn B.

ROUND 3: Join yarn C to any ch-3 corner sp, ch 3, [2 dc/*tr*, ch 3, 3 dc/*tr*] into same sp, *ch 1, 3 dc/*tr* into ch 1 sp, ch 1, **[3 dc/*tr*, ch 3, 3 dc/*tr*] into next ch-3 corner sp; rep from * twice and from * to ** once again, join with sl st into 3rd of ch-3. Break off yarn C.

ROUND 4: Join yarn D to any ch-3 corner sp, ch 3, [2 dc/*tr*, ch 3, 3 dc/*tr*] into same sp, *[ch 1, 3 dc/*tr*] into each ch-1 sp along side of square, ch 1, **[3 dc/*tr*, ch 3, 3 dc/*tr*] into next ch-3 corner sp; rep from * twice and from * to ** once again, join with sl st into 3rd of ch-3. Break off yarn D.

ROUND 5: Join yarn E to any ch-3 corner sp, ch 3, [2 dc/*tr*, ch 3, 3 dc/*tr*] into same sp, *[ch 1, 3 dc/*tr*] into each ch-1 sp along side of square, ch 1, **[3 dc/*tr*, ch 3, 3 dc/*tr*] into next ch-3 corner sp; rep from * twice and from * to ** once again, join with sl st into 3rd of ch-3. Break off yarn E.

ROUND 6: Join yarn F to any ch-3 corner sp, ch 3, [2 dc/*tr*, ch 3, 3 dc/*tr*] into same sp, *[ch 1, 3 dc/*tr*] into each ch-1 sp along side of square, ch 1, **[3 dc/*tr*, ch 3, 3 dc/*tr*] into next ch-3 corner sp; rep from * twice and from * to ** once again, join with sl st into 3rd of ch-3. Break off yarn F.

ROUND 7: Join yarn C to any ch-3 corner sp, ch 3 (counts as 1 dc/*tr*), [2 dc/*tr*, ch 3, 3 dc/*tr*] into same sp, *[ch 1, 3 dc/*tr*] into each ch-1 sp along side of square, ch 1, **[3 dc/*tr*, ch 3, 3 dc/*tr*] into next ch-3 corner sp; rep from * twice and from * to ** once again, join with sl st into 3rd of ch-3. Fasten off yarn.

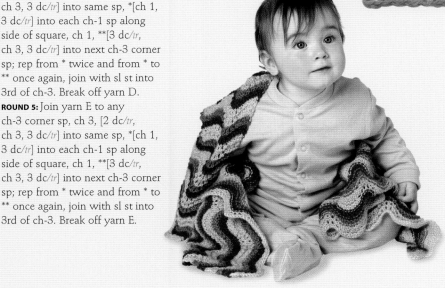

37 Lovely lace

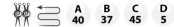

A	B	C	D
40	37	45	5

Using yarn A, CO a multiple of 12 sts plus 2.

ROW 1: (WS) K1, P to last st, K1.

ROW 2: K1, *K2tog, K2, YO, K1, YO, K2, ssk, P1, K1, P1; rep from * to last st, K1.

ROWS 3 & 5: Rep Row 1.

ROW 4: K1, *K2tog, K1, YO, K3, YO, K1, ssk, P1, K1, P1; rep from * to last st, K1.

ROW 6: K1, *K2tog, YO, K5, YO, ssk, P1, K1, P1; rep from * to last st, K1.

Rep Rows 1–6, changing yarns in the following colour sequence: 6 rows in yarn A, 6 rows in yarn B, 6 rows in yarn C, 6 rows in yarn D.

Repeat for length required.

BO/CO.

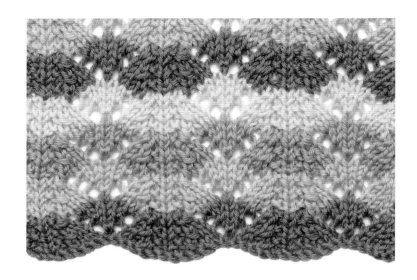

38 Grandma's square

 45

SPECIAL ABBREVIATION:

INC = increase by knitting into front and back of indicated stitch.

CO 1 st.

Beg increase pattern.

ROW 1: (RS) Inc in st on needle. (2 sts)

ROW 2: [Inc into next stitch] twice. (4 sts)

ROW 3: K4.

ROW 4: Sl 1, K1, YO, K to end of row.

Rep Row 4 until 45 sts are on the needle, ending with a WS row.

Beg decrease pattern.

ROW 1: Sl 1, K2tog, YO, K2tog, K to end of row.

Rep Row 1 until 4 sts rem on needle.

K 1 row.

NEXT ROW: [K2tog] twice. (2 sts)

NEXT ROW: K2tog.

Fasten off yarn.

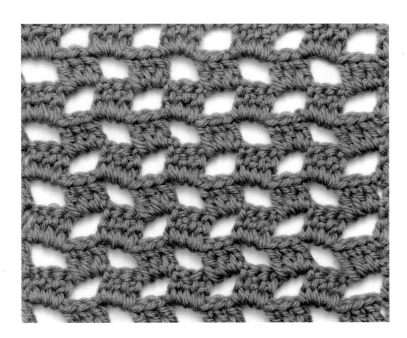

39 Tilted blocks

 39

NOTE: Either side can be used as RS.

FOUNDATION CHAIN: Work a multiple of 11 chains plus 1.

ROW 1: 1 dc/*tr* into 4th ch from hook, 1 dc/*tr* into each of next 2 chs, *ch 3, sk next 3 chs, 1 dc/*tr* into each of next 3 chs; rep from * to last 4 chs, ch 3, sk next 3 chs, 1 dc/*tr* into last ch, turn.

ROW 2: Ch 3 (counts as 1 dc/*tr*), *3 dc/*tr* into next ch-3 sp, ch 3; rep from * ending with 1 dc/*tr* into 3rd of beg skipped ch-3, turn.

ROW 3: Ch 3, *3 dc/*tr* into next ch-3 sp, ch 3; rep from * ending with 1 dc/*tr* into 3rd of ch-3, turn. Rep Row 3 for length required. Fasten off yarn.

40 Foursquare

11 [icon] **A** 39 **B** 5 **C** 6

SPECIAL ABBREVIATONS:

BEG PC = beginning popcorn made from ch 3 and 3 dc/*tr* sts.

PC = popcorn made from 4 dc/*tr* sts.

FOUNDATION RING: Using yarn A, ch 4 and join with sl st to form a ring.

ROUND 1: Beg pc into ring, [ch 3, pc into ring] three times, ch 3, join with sl st into top of beg pc.

ROUND 2: Sl st into next ch-3 sp, ch 3 (counts as 1 dc/*tr*), [2 dc/*tr*, ch 3, 3 dc/*tr*] into same ch-3 sp, ch 1, *[3 dc/*tr*, ch 3, 3 dc/*tr*] into next ch-3 sp, ch 1; rep from * twice, join with sl st into 3rd of ch-3.

ROUND 3: Ch 3, sk first dc/*tr*, 1 dc/*tr* into each rem dc/*tr* and ch-1 sp of previous round, working 5 dc/*tr* into each ch-3 corner sp; join with sl st into 3rd of ch-3.

ROUND 4: Ch 1, 1 sc/*dc* into same place, 1 sc/*dc* into each dc/*tr* of previous round, working 3 sc/*dc* into centre st of 5 dc/*tr* group at each corner, join with sl st into first sc/*dc*.

Fasten off yarn.

Make one more block in yarn A and one block in each of yarns B and C.

Using the photograph as a guide to position, stitch the four blocks together using matching yarn.

41 Textured triangles

CO a multiple of 11 stitches plus 2.

ROW 1: (RS) K1, *P1, K10; rep from * to last st, K1.

ROW 2: K1, *P9, K2; rep from * to last st, K1.

ROW 3: K1, *P3, K8; rep from * to last st, K1.

ROW 4: K1, *P7, K4; rep from * to last st, K1.

ROWS 5, 6 & 7: K1, *P5, K6; rep from * to last st, K1.

ROW 8: Rep Row 4.

ROW 9: Rep Row 3.

ROW 10: Rep Row 2.

ROW 11: Rep Row 1.

ROW 12: K1, *K1, P10; rep from * to last st, K1.

ROW 13: K1, *K9, P2; rep from * to last st, K1.

ROW 14: K1, *K3, P8; rep from * to last st, K1.

ROW 15: K1, *K7, P4; rep from * to last st, K1.

ROWS 16, 17 & 18: K1, *K5, P6; rep from * to last st, K1.

ROW 19: Rep Row 15.

ROW 20: Rep Row 14.

ROW 21: Rep Row 13.

ROW 22: Rep Row 12.

Rep Rows 1–22 for length required.

BO/*CO*.

- ☐ K ON RS ROWS, P ON WS ROW
- ☐ K ON BOTH RS AND WS ROWS
- ▨ P ON RS ROWS, K ON WS ROWS

43 Pink kiss

CO 33 sts.

Starting at the bottom right-hand corner of the chart, work the 45-row pattern from the chart, reading odd-numbered (RS) rows from right to left and even-numbered (WS) rows from left to right.

BO/*CO*.

42 Tricolour stripes

| A 32 | B 21 | C 19 |

NOTE: At colour changes, don't break off yarn, but carry colour not in use up side of work.

FOUNDATION CHAIN: Using yarn A, work any number of chains.

ROW 1: (RS) 1 sc/*dc* into 2nd ch from hook, 1 sc/*dc* into each ch to end, turn.

ROW 2: Ch 1, 1 sc/*dc* into each sc/*dc* of previous row, turn.

Rep Row 2, changing yarns in the following colour sequence:

1 row in yarn A, 1 row in yarn B, 1 row in yarn C.

Repeat for length required.

Fasten off yarn.

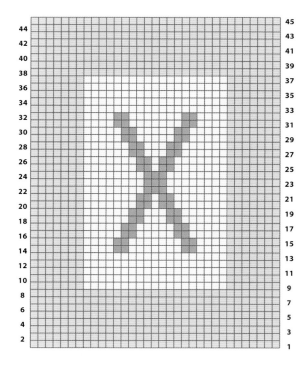

44 Wagon wheel

A	B	C	D	E	F
25	27	32	18	31	26

FOUNDATION RING: Using yarn A, ch 8 and join with sl st to form a ring.

ROUND 1: Ch 3 (counts as 1 dc/*tr*), 15 dc/*tr* into ring, join with sl st into 3rd of ch-3. (16 dc/*tr*) Break off yarn A.

ROUND 2: Join yarn B to any dc/*tr* of previous round, ch 5 (counts as 1 dc/*tr*, ch 2), [1 dc/*tr* into next dc/*tr*, ch 2] 15 times, join with sl st into 3rd of ch-5. (16 spaced dc/*tr*) Break off yarn B.

ROUND 3: Join yarn C to any ch-2 sp, ch 3 (counts as 1 dc/*tr*), 2 dc/*tr* into same sp, ch 1, *[3 dc/*tr*, ch 1] into next ch-2 sp; rep from * to end, join with sl st into 3rd of ch-3. Break off yarn C.

ROUND 4: Join yarn D to any ch-1 sp, 1 sc/*dc* into same sp, *[ch 3, 1 sc/*dc* into next ch-1 sp] three times, ch 6 to make corner sp, **1 sc/*dc* into next ch-1 sp; rep from * twice and from * to ** once more, join with sl st into first of ch-3.

ROUND 5: Sl st into next ch-3 sp, ch 3, 2 dc/*tr* into same sp, 3 dc/*tr* into each of next two ch-3 sps, *[5 dc/*tr*, ch 2, 5 dc/*tr*] into ch-6 corner sp, **3 dc/*tr* into each of next three ch-3 sps; rep from * to last ch-6 corner sp and rep from * to ** once more, join with sl st into 3rd of ch-3. Break off yarn D.

ROUND 6: Join yarn E to any dc/*tr* along side of square, ch 3, 1 dc/*tr* into each dc/*tr* of previous round, working [1 dc/*tr*, 1 tr/*dtr*, 1 dc/*tr*] into each ch-2 corner sp, join with sl st into 3rd of ch-3. Break off yarn E.

ROUND 7: Join yarn F to any dc/*tr* along side of square, ch 3, 1 dc/*tr* into every dc/*tr* of previous round, working 5 dc/*tr* into tr/*dtr* at each corner, join with sl st into 3rd of ch-3. Fasten off yarn.

45 Offset daisy

A 4 **B 42** **C 49**

FOUNDATION RING: Using yarn A, ch 6 and join with sl st to form a ring.

ROUND 1: Ch 3 (counts as 1 dc/*tr*), 15 dc/*tr* into ring, join with sl st into 3rd of ch-3.

ROUND 2: Ch 5 (counts as 1 dc/*tr*, ch 2), [1 dc/*tr* into next dc/*tr*, ch 2] 15 times, join with sl st into 3rd of ch-5. Break off yarn A.

ROUND 3: Join yarn B to any ch-2 sp, ch 3, [1 dc/*tr*, ch 2, 2 dc/*tr*] into same sp, *[ch 2, 1 sc/*dc* into next ch-2 sp] three times, ch 2, **[2 dc/*tr*, ch 2, 2 dc/*tr*] into next ch-2 sp; rep from * twice and from * to ** once more, join with sl st into 3rd of ch-3.

ROUND 4: Ch 3, 1 dc/*tr* into next dc/*tr*, *[1 dc/*tr*, 1 tr/*dtr*, 1 dc/*tr*] into next ch-2 sp to make corner, 1 dc/*tr* into each of next 2 dc/*tr*, [2 dc/*tr* into next ch-2 sp, 1 dc/*tr* into next

sc/*dc*] three times, 2 dc/*tr* into next ch-2 sp, **1 dc/*tr* into each of next 2 dc/*tr*; rep from * twice and from * to ** once more, join with sl st into 3rd of ch-3. Break off yarn B. Change from working in rounds to working in rows.

ROW 1: With RS of square facing, join yarn C to tr/*dtr* at any corner, ch 1, 1 sc/*dc* into same tr/*dtr*, 1 sc/*dc* into each dc/*tr* along side of square, 3 sc/*dc* into next tr/*dtr* at corner, 1 sc/*dc* into each dc/*tr* along next side of square, 1 sc/*dc* into next tr/*dtr* at corner, turn.

ROW 2: Ch 3 (counts as 1 dc/*tr*), sk first sc/*dc*, 1 dc/*tr* into each sc/*dc* of previous row, working 3 dc/*tr* into centre st of 3 dc/*tr* group at corner, turn.

ROW 3: Ch 3, sk first dc/*tr*, 1 dc/*tr* into each dc/*tr* of previous round, working 3 dc/*tr* into centre st of

3 dc/*tr* group at corner and working last dc/*tr* of row into 3rd of ch-3.

ROW 4: Rep Row 3.

Break off yarn C. Join yarn B.

ROWS 5 & 6: Rep Row 3. Fasten off yarn.

46 All yellow

 4

FOUNDATION CHAIN: Work a multiple of 3 chains plus 1.

ROW 1: (RS) 1 dc/*tr* into 4th ch from hook, *sk next 2 chs, 3 dc/*tr* into next ch; rep from * ending last rep with 2 dc/*tr* into last ch, turn.

ROW 2: Ch 3 (counts as 1 dc/*tr*), sk first dc/*tr*, 1 dc/*tr* into next dc/*tr*, *ch 2, dc3tog/*tr3tog*; rep from * ending last rep with 1 dc/*tr* into next dc/*tr*, 1 dc/*tr* into 3rd of beg skipped ch-3, turn.

ROW 3: Ch 3, 3 dc/*tr* into first ch-3 sp, *3 dc/*tr* into next ch-3 sp; rep from * ending with 1 dc/*tr* into 3rd of ch-3, turn.

ROW 4: Ch 4 (counts as 1 dc/*tr*, ch 1), sk first dc/*tr*, dc3tog/*tr3tog*, *ch 2, dc3tog/*tr3tog*; rep from * ending with ch 1, 1 dc/*tr* into 3rd of ch-3, turn.

ROW 5: Ch 3, 1 dc/*tr* into first dc/*tr*, *3 dc/*tr* into next ch-2 sp; rep from * ending with 2 dc/*tr* into 3rd of ch-4, turn.

ROW 6: Ch 3, sk first dc/*tr*, 1 dc/*tr* into next dc/*tr*, *ch 2, dc3tog/*tr3tog*; rep from * ending last rep with 1 dc/*tr* into next dc/*tr*, 1 dc/*tr* into 3rd of ch-3, turn.

Rep Rows 3–6 for length required. Fasten off yarn.

Red squares

CO 33 sts.
Starting at the bottom right-hand corner of the chart, work the 45-row pattern from the chart, reading odd-numbered (RS) rows from right to left and even-numbered (WS) rows from left to right.
BO/CO.

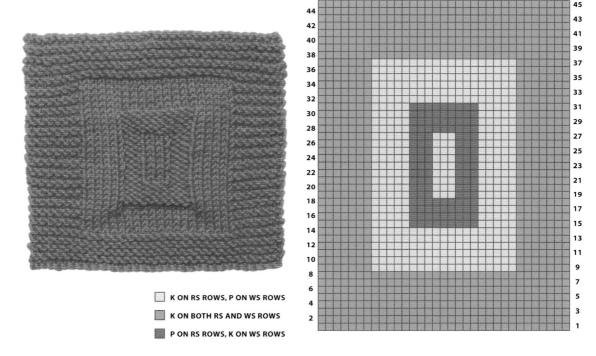

- ☐ K ON RS ROWS, P ON WS ROWS
- ▨ K ON BOTH RS AND WS ROWS
- ▨ P ON RS ROWS, K ON WS ROWS

 Dazzler

NOTES: Slip all slipped stitches purlwise, keeping yarn on wrong side of work. At colour changes, don't break off yarn, but carry colour not in use up side of work.

Using yarn A, CO a multiple of 6 sts plus 5.
ROW 1: (RS) K2, *sl 1, K5; rep from * to last 3 sts, sl 1, K2.
ROW 2: K1, P1, sl 1, *P5, sl 1; rep from * to last 2 sts, P1, K1.
ROW 3: *K5, sl 1; rep from * to last 5 sts, K5.

ROW 4: *K5, sl 1; rep from * to last 5 sts, K5.
Rep Rows 1–4, changing yarns in the following colour sequence:
2 rows in yarn A, 2 rows in yarn B.
Rep for length required.
BO/CO.

49 Lucy's flower

A B C D
3 31 37 51

ROUND 7: Join yarn D to centre st of any 3 sc/*dc* group, ch 3, 2 dc/*tr* into same sc/*dc*, *1 hdc/*htr* into each of next 2 sc/*dc*, 1 sc/*dc* into each of next 7 sc/*dc*, 1 hdc/*htr* into each of next 2 sc/*dc*, **3 dc/*tr* into next sc/*dc*; rep from * twice and from * to ** once again, join with sl st into 3rd of ch-3.

ROUND 8: Sl st into next dc/*tr*, ch 4 (counts as 1 tr/*dtr*), 2 tr/*dtr* into same dc/*tr*, *1 dc/*tr* into each of next 2 sts, 1 hdc/*htr* into each of next 9 sts, 1 dc/*tr* into each of next 2 sts, **3 tr/*dtr* into next st; rep from * twice and from * to ** once again, join with sl st into 4th of ch-4. Break off yarn D.

ROUND 9: Join yarn B to first st of any 3 tr/*dtr* corner group, ch 1, 1 sc/*dc* into same place, *3 sc/*dc* into next tr/*dtr*, 1 sc/*dc* into each of next 15 sts; rep from * three times, ending last rep with 1 sc/*dc* into each of next 14 sts, join with sl st into first sc/*dc*.

ROUND 10: Ch 1, 1 sc/*dc* into each sc/*dc* of previous round, working 3 sc/*dc* into centre st of each 3 sc/*dc* corner group, join with sl st into first sc/*dc*.

ROUND 11: Ch 3 (counts as 1 dc/*tr*), 1 dc/*tr* into each sc/*dc* of previous round, working [2 dc/*tr*, ch 2, 2 dc/*tr*] into centre st of each 3 sc/*dc* corner group, join with sl st into 3rd of ch-3.

ROUND 12: Ch 1, 1 sc/*dc* into each dc/*tr* of previous round, working 3 sc/*dc* into each ch-2 corner sp, join with sl st into first sc/*dc*. Fasten off yarn.

SPECIAL ABBREVIATIONS:

BEG CL = beginning cluster made from 1 dc/*tr* st.

CL = cluster made from 2 dc/*tr* sts.

FOUNDATION RING: Using yarn A, ch 4 and join with sl st to form a ring.

ROUND 1: Ch 1, 6 sc/*dc* into ring, join with sl st into first sc/*dc*.

ROUND 2: Ch 1, 2 sc/*dc* into next sc/*dc* six times, join with sl st into first sc/*dc*. Break off yarn A.

ROUND 3: Join yarn B to any sc/*dc*, ch 1, 2 sc/*dc* into next sc/*dc* 12 times, join with sl st into first sc/*dc*.

ROUND 4: Ch 3, beg CL into same sc/*dc*, ch 2, sk next sc/*dc*, *CL into next sc/*dc*, ch 2, sk next sc/*dc*; rep from * ten times, join with sl st in top of beg CL. Break off yarn B.

ROUND 5: Join yarn C to any ch-2 sp, ch 3, beg CL into same sp, ch 3, *CL into next ch-2 sp, ch 3; rep from * ten times, join with sl st into top of beg CL.

ROUND 6: Ch 1, 1 sc/*dc* into top of beg CL, 3 sc/*dc* into next ch-3 sp, *1 sc/*dc* into top of next CL, 3 sc/*dc* into next ch-3 sp; rep from * ten times, join with sl st into first sc/*dc*. Break off yarn C.

50 Candy stripe

NOTE: At colour changes, do not break yarn, but carry colour not in use up side of work.

Using yarn A, CO 61 sts and K 1 row.

ROW 1: (RS) K29, sl 1, K2tog, psso, K29.

ROW 2: K.

ROW 3: K28, sl 1, K2tog, psso, K28.

ROW 4: K.
Join yarn B.

ROW 5: K27, sl 1, K2tog, psso, K27.

ROW 6: K.
Cont working in this way, dec 2 sts at centre of every RS (odd-numbered) row and working 4 rows in yarn A, 2 rows in yarn B until 3 sts rem on needle, ending with a WS row.

NEXT ROW: K3tog.
Fasten off yarn.

52 Baby mesh

FOUNDATION CHAIN: Work a multiple of 2 chains.

ROW 1: (RS) 1 sc/*dc* into 2nd ch from hook, *ch 1, sk next ch, 1 sc/*dc* into next ch; rep from * to end, turn.

ROW 2: Ch 1, 1 sc/*dc* into first sc/*dc*, *ch 1, 1 sc/*dc* into next sc/*dc*; rep from * to end, turn.
Rep Row 2 for length required.
Fasten off yarn.

51 Pastel ripple

NOTE: Where possible, do not break yarn at colour changes, instead carry yarn not in use up side of work.

Using yarn A, CO a multiple of 13 stitches plus 3.

ROW 1: (RS) K1, *K1, YO, K4, K2tog, sl 1, K1, psso, K4, YO; rep from * to last st, K2.

ROW 2: K1, P to last st, K1.
Rep Rows 1 & 2, changing yarns in the following colour sequence: 6 rows in yarn A, 2 rows in yarn B, 2 rows in yarn A, 2 rows in yarn B, 6 rows in yarn A, 2 rows in yarn C, 2 rows in yarn A, 2 rows in yarn C. Repeat for length required.
BO/*CO*.

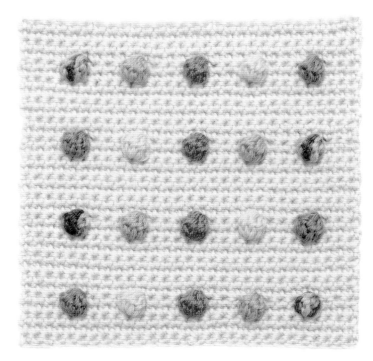

53 Lavender bobbles

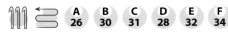

SPECIAL ABBREVIATION:

MB = Using a separate length of yarn in the colour indicated, make bobble (keeping last loop of each stitch on hook, work 5 dc/*tr* into same stitch, YO and draw yarn through all 6 loops).

FOUNDATION CHAIN: Ch 30.

ROW 1: (WS) 1 sc/*dc* into 2nd ch from hook, 1 sc/*dc* into each ch to end, turn. (29 sc/*dc*)

ROW 2: Ch 1, 1 sc/*dc* into each sc/*dc* to end, turn.

ROWS 3 & 4: Rep Row 2.

ROW 5: Ch 1, 1 sc/*dc* into each of next 4 sc/*dc*, MB in B, 1 sc/*dc* into each of next 4 sc/*dc*, MB in C, 1 sc/*dc* into each of next 4 sc/*dc*, MB in D, 1 sc/*dc* into each of next 4 sc/*dc*, MB in E, 1 sc/*dc* into each of next 4 sc/*dc*, MB in F, 1 sc/*dc* into each of next 4 sc/*dc*, turn.

ROWS 6–12: Rep Row 2.

ROW 13: Ch 1, 1 sc/*dc* into each of next 4 sc/*dc*, MB in F, 1 sc/*dc* into each of next 4 sc/*dc*, MB in E, 1 sc/*dc* into each of next 4 sc/*dc*, MB in D, 1 sc/*dc* into each of next 4 sc/*dc*, MB in C, 1 sc/*dc* into each of next 4 sc/*dc*, MB in B, 1 sc/*dc* into each of next 4 sc/*dc*, turn.

ROWS 14–20: Rep Row 2.

ROW 21: Rep Row 5.

ROWS 22–28: Rep Row 2.

ROW 29: Rep Row 13.

ROWS 30–33: Rep Row 2.

Fasten off yarn.

54 All-over stripes

SPECIAL ABBREVIATION:

INC = increase by knitting into front and back of indicated stitch.

NOTE: At colour changes, don't break main yarn, instead carry it loosely up side of work.

Using yarn A, CO 1 st and inc in this st. (2 sts)

Beg increase pattern.

ROW 1: (WS) K1, inc in last st.

ROW 2: K2, inc in last st.

ROW 3: K to last st, inc in last st.

Rep Row 3 until there are 43 sts on needle, ending with a WS row. At the same time, change colours in the following sequence:

2 rows in yarn B, 4 rows in yarn A, 2 rows in yarn C, 2 rows in yarn A, 2 rows in yarn D, 6 rows in yarn A, 4 rows in yarn C, 2 rows in yarn A, 2 rows in yarn C, 4 rows in yarn A, 4 rows in yarn B, 2 rows in yarn A, 2 rows in yarn D.

NEXT ROW: Using yarn A, K. Beg decrease pattern.

ROW 43: Using yarn A, K to last 2 sts, K2tog.

Cont to decrease 1 st at end of every row as set, changing colours in the following sequence:

2 rows in yarn C, 10 rows in yarn A, 4 rows in yarn D, 2 rows in yarn A, 2 rows in yarn C. Break off yarn C and cont as set in yarn A until 2 sts rem on needle, ending with a WS row.

NEXT ROW: K2tog.

Fasten off yarn.

55 Mini flowers

  66

REPEAT SIZE: 6 blocks high by 6 blocks wide.

NOTE: The flower pattern repeats across the mesh background. Alternatively, scatter individual flower shapes at random across the mesh background.

WORKING THE REPEAT PATTERN: Begin working the pattern from the chart, repeating the section of the chart inside the red lines. Starting at the bottom right-hand corner of the chart, work the blocks and spaces from the chart in filet crochet (page 121). When following the chart, read odd-numbered (RS) rows from right to left and even-numbered (WS) rows from left to right. Fasten off yarn.

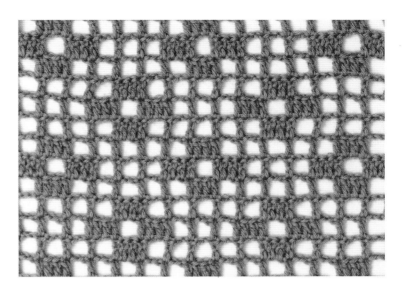

56 Travelling vines

 31

CO a multiple of 9 sts plus 4.

ROW 1 AND EVERY ALT ROW: (WS) K1, P to last st, K1.

ROW 2: K3, *YO, K2, sl 1, K1, psso, K2tog, K2, YO, K1; rep from * to last st, K1.

ROW 4: K2, *YO, K2, sl 1, K1, psso, K2tog, K2, YO, K1; rep from * to last 2 sts, K2.

Rep Rows 1–4 for length required. BO/CO.

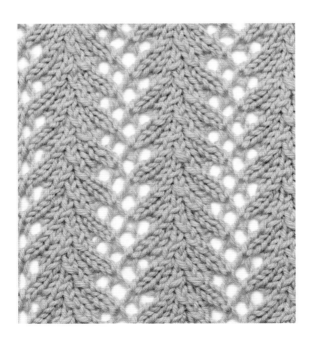

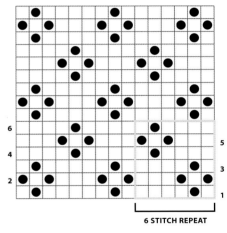

6 STITCH REPEAT

☐ SPACE

● BLOCK

57 Colourful square

   A 52 **B 21**

FOUNDATION RING: Using yarn A, ch 4 and join with sl st to form a ring.

ROUND 1: Ch 3 (counts as 1 dc/*tr*), 11 dc/*tr* into ring, join with sl st into 3rd of ch-3. (12 dc/*tr*)

ROUND 2: Ch 3, *[2 dc/*tr*, 1 tr/*dtr*] into next dc/*tr*, [1 tr/*dtr*, 2 dc/*tr*] into next dc/*tr*, **1 dc/*tr* into next dc/*tr*; rep from * twice and from * to ** once again, join with sl st into 3rd of ch-3.

ROUND 3: Ch 3, 1 dc/*tr* into each of next 2 dc/*tr*, *[2 dc/*tr*, 1 tr/*dtr*] into next tr/*dtr*, [1 tr/*dtr*, 2 dc/*tr*] into next tr/*dtr*, **1 dc/*tr* into each of next 5 dc/*tr*; rep from * twice and from * to ** once again, 1 dc/*tr* into

each of next 2 dc/*tr*, join with sl st into 3rd of ch-3.

ROUND 4: Ch 3, 1 dc/*tr* into each of next 4 dc/*tr*, *[2 dc/*tr*, 1 tr/*dtr*] into next tr/*dtr*, [1 tr/*dtr*, 2 dc/*tr*] into next tr/*dtr*, **1 dc/*tr* into each of next 9 dc/*tr*; rep from * twice and from * to ** once again, 1 dc/*tr* into each of next 4 dc/*tr*, join with sl st into 3rd of ch-3.

ROUND 5: Ch 3, 1 dc/*tr* into each of next 6 dc/*tr*, *[2 dc/*tr*, 1 tr/*dtr*] into next tr/*dtr*, [1 tr/*dtr*, 2 dc/*tr*] into next tr/*dtr*, **1 dc/*tr* into each of next 13 dc/*tr*; rep from * twice and from * to ** once again, 1 dc/*tr* into each of next 6 dc/*tr*, join with sl st

into 3rd of ch-3. Break off yarn A.

ROUND 6: Join yarn B, ch 3, 1 dc/*tr* into each of next 8 dc/*tr*, *[2 dc/*tr*, 1 tr/*dtr*] into next tr/*dtr*, [1 tr/*dtr*, 2 dc/*tr*] into next tr/*dtr*, **1 dc/*tr* into each of next 17 dc/*tr*; rep from * twice and from * to ** once again, 1 dc/*tr* into each of next 8 dc/*tr*, join with sl st into 3rd of ch-3.

ROUND 7: Ch 1, 1 sc/*dc* into same place, 1 sc/*dc* into each dc/*tr* of previous round, working [2 sc/*dc*, 1 hdc/*htr*] into first tr/*dtr* of each corner group and [1 hdc/*htr*, 2 sc/*dc*] into last tr/*dtr* of each corner group, join with sl st into first sc/*dc*. Fasten off yarn.

58 Sunny scallops

   4

SPECIAL ABBREVIATION:

SSK = slip, slip, knit (slip next two stitches one at a time, insert left needle into fronts of slipped stitches and knit them together). Slip all stitches knitwise.

CO a multiple of 13 sts plus 2.

ROW 1: (RS) K1, *ssk, K9, K2tog; rep from * to last st, K1.

ROW 2: K1, P to last st, K1.

ROW 3: K1, *ssk, K7, K2tog; rep from * to last st, K1.

ROW 4: Rep Row 2.

ROW 5: K1, *ssk, [YO, K1] five times, YO, K2tog; rep from * to last st, K1.

ROW 6: K.

Rep Rows 1–6 for length required. BO/*CO*.

59 Cheeky stripes

A	B	C	D	E	F	G	H
32	52	45	7	39	4	48	21

NOTE: At colour changes on each block, don't break off yarn, but carry colour not in use up side of work.

BLOCK 1
Using yarn A, CO 31 sts and K 1 row.
ROW 1: (RS) K14, sl 1, K2tog, psso, K14.
ROW 2: K.
ROW 3: Using yarn B, K13, sl 1, K2tog, psso, K13.
ROW 4: K.
Cont working in this way, dec 2 sts at the centre of every RS (odd-numbered) row and working two-row stripes in alternate colours until 3 sts remain on the needle, ending with a WS row.
NEXT ROW: K3tog.
Fasten off yarn.

BLOCK 2
Work as Block 1 using yarn C instead of yarn A, yarn D instead of yarn B.

BLOCK 3
Work as Block 1 using yarn E instead of yarn A, yarn F instead of yarn B.

BLOCK 4
Work as Block 1 using yarn G instead of yarn A, yarn H instead of yarn B.

Using the photograph as a guide to position, join the cast-on edges of the four blocks together using the overcasting method of joining shown on page 116.

60 Blue shells

 39

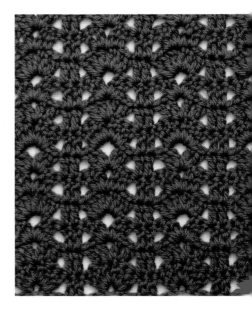

FOUNDATION CHAIN: Using yarn A, work a multiple of 7 chains plus 4.
ROW 1: (WS) 1 dc/*tr* into 4th ch from hook, *sk next 2 chs, [3 dc/*tr*, ch 1, 3 dc/*tr*] into next ch, sk next 2 chs, 1 dc/*tr* into each of next 2 chs; rep from * to end, turn.
ROW 2: Ch 3, sk first dc/*tr*, 1 dc/*tr* into next dc/*tr*, *sk next 2 dc/*tr*, 1 dc/*tr* into next dc/*tr*, ch 1, [1 dc/*tr*, ch 1, 1 dc/*tr*] into next ch-1 sp, ch 1, 1 dc/*tr* into next dc/*tr*, sk next 2 dc/*tr*, 1 dc/*tr* into each of next 2 dc/*tr*; rep from * to end working

last dc/*tr* into 3rd of beg skipped ch-3, turn.
ROW 3: Ch 3, sk first dc/*tr*, 1 dc/*tr* into next dc/*tr*, *sk next ch-1 sp, [2 dc/*tr*, ch 3, 2 dc/*tr*] into next ch-1 sp, sk next 2 dc/*tr*, 1 dc/*tr* into each of next 2 dc/*tr*; rep from * to end working last dc/*tr* into 3rd of ch-3.
ROW 4: Ch 3, sk first dc/*tr*, 1 dc/*tr* into next dc/*tr*, *[3 dc/*tr*, ch 1, 3 dc/*tr*] into next ch-3 sp, sk next 2 dc/*tr*, 1 dc/*tr* into each of next 2 dc/*tr*; rep from * to end working last dc/*tr* into 3rd of ch-3.

ROW 5: Ch 3, sk first dc/*tr*, 1 dc/*tr* into next dc/*tr*, *sk next 2 dc/*tr*, 1 dc/*tr* into next dc/*tr*, ch 1, [1 dc/*tr*, ch 1, 1 dc/*tr*] into next ch-1 sp, ch 1, 1 dc/*tr* into next dc/*tr*, sk next 2 dc/*tr*, 1 dc/*tr* into each of next 2 dc/*tr*; rep from * to end working last dc/*tr* into 3rd of ch-3, turn.
Rep Rows 3–5 for length required.
Fasten off yarn.

61 Pot pourri

 A 50 B 20 C 21 D 16 E 23

BACKGROUND BLOCK
FOUNDATION CHAIN: Using yarn A, ch 29.
ROW 1: (RS) 1 sc/*dc* into 2nd ch from hook, 1 sc/*dc* into each ch to end, turn. (28 sc/*dc*)
ROW 2: Ch 1, 1 sc/*dc* into each sc/*dc* of previous row, turn.
Rep Row 2 32 times more, ending with a WS row.
Fasten off yarn.

FLOWER MOTIFS (MAKE 4)
FOUNDATION RING: Using yarn B, ch 6 and join with sl st to form a ring.
ROUND 1: Ch 3 (counts as 1 dc/*tr*), 3 dc/*tr* into ring, ch 3, turn; 1 dc/*tr* into first dc/*tr*, 1 dc/*tr* into each of next 2 dc/*tr*, 1 dc/*tr* into

3rd of ch-3 (petal made), ch 3, turn; * working across back of petal just made, work 4 dc/*tr* into ring, ch 3, turn; 1 dc/*tr* into first dc/*tr*, 1 dc/*tr* into each of next 3 dc/*tr* (petal made), ch 3, turn; rep from * 4 times more, join round with sl st to 3rd of beg ch-3 of first petal.
Fasten off yarn, leaving a long tail for stitching motif to background. Make one flower using yarns C, D and E.
After blocking, pin flower motifs to background block using photograph as a guide to placement. Stitch each motif in place with yarn tail, stitching over the chains beneath each petal.

62 Lattice lace

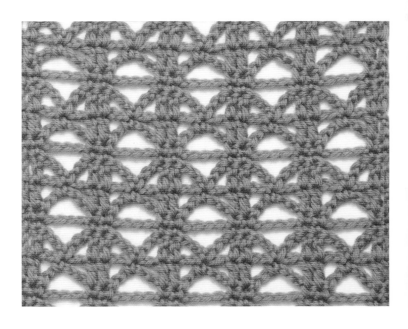

FOUNDATION CHAIN: Work a multiple of 6 chains plus 3.
ROW 1: (RS) 1 sc/*dc* into 2nd ch from hook, 1 sc/*dc* into next ch, *ch 6, sk next 4 chs, 1 sc/*dc* into each of next 2 chs; rep from * to end, turn.
ROW 2: Ch 3 (counts as 1 dc/*tr*), sk first sc/*dc*, 1 dc/*tr* into next sc/*dc*, *ch 2, 1 sc/*dc* into ch-6 sp, ch 2, 1 dc/*tr* into each of next 2 sc/*dc*; rep from * to end, turn.
ROW 3: Ch 3, sk first dc/*tr*, 1 dc/*tr* into next dc/*tr*, *ch 3, sl st into next sc/*dc*, ch 3, 1 dc/*tr* into each of next 2 dc/*tr*; rep from

* working last dc/*tr* into 3rd of ch-3, turn.
ROW 4: Ch 1, 1 sc/*dc* into each of first 2 dc/*tr*, *ch 4, 1 sc/*dc* into each of next 2 dc/*tr*; rep from * working last dc/*tr* into 3rd of ch-3, turn.
ROW 5: Ch 1, 1 sc/*dc* into each of first 2 sc/*dc*, *ch 6, 1 sc/*dc* into each of next 2 sc/*dc*; rep from * to end, turn.
Rep Rows 2–5 for length required. Fasten off yarn.

63 Matilda

NOTES: Slip all stitches purlwise keeping yarn on wrong side of work. Don't break yarn at colour changes, instead carry colour not in use loosely up side of work.

Using yarn A, CO a multiple of 2 sts plus 2.
ROW 1: (RS) K.
ROW 2: Rep Row 1.
ROW 3: K1, *K1, sl 1; rep from * to last st, K1.
ROW 4: K1, P to last st, K1.
ROWS 5 & 6: Rep Row 1.
ROW 7: K1, *sl 1, K1; rep from * to last st, K1.
ROW 8: K1, P to last st, K1.
Rep Rows 1–8, changing yarns in the following colour sequence:
2 rows in yarn A, 4 rows in yarn B, 2 rows in yarn A.
Repeat for length required.
BO/CO.

64 Textured heart

CO 33 sts.
Starting at the bottom right-hand corner of the chart, work the 43-row pattern from the chart, reading odd-numbered (RS) rows from right to left and even-numbered (WS) rows from left to right.
BO/CO.

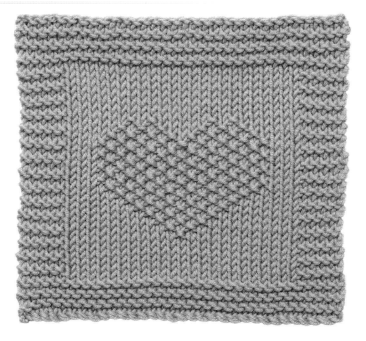

☐ K ON RS ROWS, P ON WS ROWS

☐ K ON BOTH RS AND WS ROWS

▨ P ON RS ROWS, K ON WS ROWS

 65 # Summer sun

     A 57 **B 4**

BACKGROUND BLOCK
Using yarn A, CO 33 sts.
ROW 1: (RS) * K1, P1; rep from * to last st, K1.
ROWS 2 , 3 & 4: Rep Row 1.
ROW 5: [K1, P1] twice, K25, [P1, K1] twice.
ROW 6: [K1, P1] twice, P25, [P1, K1] twice.
Rep Rows 5 & 6 16 times more, ending with a Row 6.
Rep Rows 1–4 once more.
BO/CO.

SUN MOTIF
Using yarn B, CO 8 sts.
ROW 1: (WS) K.
ROW 2: K2, YO, K2, turn without working rem 4 stitches on left-hand needle.

ROW 3: K5.
ROW 4: K2, YO, K5, turn without working rem 2 stitches on left-hand needle.
ROW 5: K8.
ROW 6: BO/CO 2 sts, K rem 7 sts.
Rep Rows 1–6 17 times more, ending with a Row 6.
BO/CO.
Join CO and BO/CO edges together. Work a row of running stitches round inner circle, pull to close circle and fasten off yarn. After blocking, use matching yarn to stitch sun motif to centre of background block, stitching between each ray.

66 # Popcorn quartet

 **A 57** **B 6** **C 7** **D 59** **E 58**

SPECIAL ABBREVIATION:
PC = popcorn made from 5 dc/*tr* sts.

FOUNDATION RING: Using yarn A, ch 4 and join with sl st to form a ring.
ROUND 1: Ch 3 (counts as 1 dc/*tr*), 3 dc/*tr* into ring, ch 1, [4 dc/*tr* into ring, ch 1] three times, join with sl st into 3rd of ch-3. Break off yarn A.
ROUND 2: Join yarn B to any ch-1 sp, ch 3, [3 dc/*tr*, ch 1, 4 dc/*tr*] into same ch-1 sp, ch 1, *[4 dc/*tr*, ch 1, 4 dc/*tr*] into next ch-1 sp, ch 1; rep from * twice, join with sl st into 3rd of ch-3. Break off yarn B.
ROUND 3: Join yarn C to any ch-1 corner sp, ch 3, [1 dc/*tr*, pc, 2 dc/*tr*] into same sp, (sk next dc/*tr*,

1 dc/*tr* into each of next 3 dc/*tr*, 1 dc/*tr* into ch-1 sp, 1 dc/*tr* into each of next 3 dc/*tr*, sk next dc/*tr*, **[2 dc/*tr*, pc, 2 dc/*tr*] into next ch-1 corner sp; rep from * twice and from * to ** once more, join with sl st into 3rd of ch-3.
ROUND 4: Ch 1, 1 sc/*dc* into each dc/*tr* of previous round, working 3 sc/*dc* into top of each popcorn, join with sl st into first sc/*dc*. Fasten off yarn. Work one more block using the same colour combination and two blocks using yarn D instead of yarn A and yarn E instead of yarn B. Using the photograph as a guide to position, stitch the four blocks together using matching yarn.

67 Tweedy

NOTES: Slip all stitches purlwise keeping yarn on wrong side of work. Don't break yarn at colour changes, instead carry colour not in use loosely up side of work.

Using yarn A, CO a multiple of 3 sts plus 2.

ROW 1: (RS) K1, *sl 1, K2; rep from * to last st, K1.

ROW 2: K.

ROW 3: K1, *K2, sl 1; rep from * to last st, K1.

ROW 4: K.

Rep Rows 1–4, changing yarns in the following colour sequence: 2 rows in yarn A, 2 rows in yarn B.

Repeat for length required. BO/CO.

68 Sunny windows

FOUNDATION CHAIN: Work a multiple of 2 chains plus 3.

ROW 1: (RS) 1 dc/tr into 4th ch from hook, 1 dc/tr into each ch to end, turn.

ROW 2: Ch 4 (counts as 1 dc/tr, ch 1), sk first 2 dc/tr, 1 dc/tr into next dc/tr, *ch 1, sk next dc/tr, 1 dc/tr into next dc/tr; rep from * working last dc/tr into 3rd of beg skipped ch-3, turn.

ROW 3: Ch 3 (counts as 1 dc/tr), 1 dc/tr into next ch-1 sp, 1 dc/tr into next dc/tr; rep from * to last dc/tr, 1 dc/tr into sp made by ch-4 of previous row, 1 dc/tr into 3rd of ch-4, turn.

ROW 4: Ch 4 (counts as 1 dc/tr, ch 1), sk first 2 dc/tr, 1 dc/tr into next dc/tr, *ch 1, sk next dc/tr, 1 dc/tr into next dc/tr; rep from * working last dc/tr into 3rd of ch-3, turn.

Rep Rows 3 & 4 for length required. Fasten off yarn.

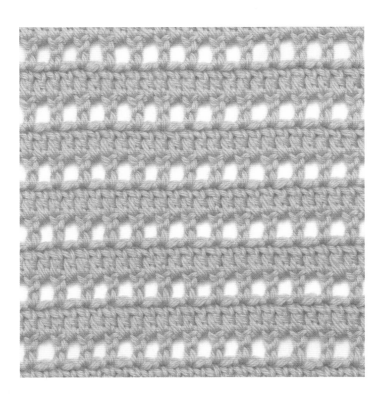

 69 # Baby panels

39

CO 33 sts.
ROW 1: (WS) K4, *P1, K3; rep from * to last st, K1.
ROW 2: *K1, P3; rep from * to last st, K1.
ROW 3: K3, P1, K1, *[P1, K2] twice, P1, K1; rep from * to last 4 sts, P1, K3.
ROW 4: K1, P2, K1, P1, *[K1, P2] twice, K1, P1; rep from * to last 4 sts, K1, P2, K1.
ROW 5: K2, *P1, K1; rep from * to last st, K1.
ROW 6: K1, *P1, K1: rep from * to end.
ROW 7: Rep Row 3.
ROW 8: Rep Row 4.
ROW 9: Rep Row 1.
ROW 10: Rep Row 2.
Rep Rows 1–10 three times more, ending with a RS row.
BO/CO.

 70 # Blue moon

A 44 **B 39** **C 45**

FOUNDATION RING: Using yarn A, ch 6 and join with sl st to form a ring.
ROUND 1: Ch 1, 16 sc/dc into ring, join with sl st to first sc/dc. (16 sc/dc)
ROUND 2: Ch 6 (counts as 1 dc/tr, ch 3), sk next sc/dc, [1 dc/tr into next sc/dc, ch 3, sk next sc/dc] seven times, join with sl st into 3rd of ch-3.
ROUND 3: Ch 1, work petal of [1 sc/dc, 1 hdc/htr, 3 tr/dtr, 1 hdc/htr, 1 sc/dc] into each of next 8 ch-3 sps, join with sl st into first sc/dc.
ROUND 4: Ch 1, [1 sc/dc between next 2 sc/dc, ch 6] eight times, join with sl st into first sc/dc.
ROUND 5: Ch 1, work petal of [1 sc/dc, 1 hdc/htr, 5 tr/dtr, 1 hdc/htr, 1 sc/dc] into each of next 8 ch-6 sps, join with sl st into first sc/dc. Break off yarn A.
ROUND 6: Join yarn B to centre st of any petal, ch 1, 1 sc/dc into same st, *ch 3, 1 dc/tr into next

sp between petals, ch 3, 1 sc/dc into centre st of next petal, ch 2, [2 tr/dtr, ch 2, 2 tr/dtr] into next sp between petals, ch 2, **1 sc/dc into centre st of next petal; rep from * twice and from * to ** once more, join with sl st into first sc/dc.
ROUND 7: Ch 3 (counts as 1 dc/tr), *3 dc/tr into next ch-3 sp, 1 dc/tr into next dc/tr, 3 dc/tr into next ch-3 sp, 1 dc/tr into next sc/dc, 2 dc/tr into next ch-2 sp, 1 dc/tr into each of next 2 tr/dtr, [3 dc/tr, ch 2, 3 dc/tr] into next ch-2 corner sp, 1 dc/tr into each of next 2 tr/dtr, 2 dc/tr into next ch-2 sp, **1 dc/tr into next sc/dc; rep from * twice and from * to ** once more, join with sl st into 3rd of ch-3. Break off yarn B.
ROUND 8: Join yarn C, ch 3, 1 dc/tr into each dc/tr of previous round, working [2 dc/tr, ch 2, 2 dc/tr] into each ch-2 corner sp, join with sl st into 3rd of ch-3. Fasten off yarn.

71 Old shale

A B C D
46 45 44 35

Using yarn A, CO a multiple of 18 sts plus 2.

ROW 1: (RS) K.
ROW 2: K1, P to last st, K1.
ROW 3: K1, *[K2tog] three times, [YO, K1] six times, [K2tog] three times; rep from * to last st, K1.
ROW 4: K.

Rep Rows 1–4, changing yarns in the following colour sequence: 4 rows in yarn A, 4 rows in yarn B, 4 rows in yarn C, 4 rows in yarn D.
Repeat for length required.
BO/CO.

72 Alternate shells

45

SPECIAL ABBREVIATIONS:
F = fan (work [3 dc/*tr*, ch 1, 3 dc/*tr*] into next chain or space).
V = v-shaped stitch (work [1 hdc/*htr*, ch 1, 1 hdc/*htr*] into next space).

FOUNDATION CHAIN: Work a multiple of 10 chains plus 2.

ROW 1: (RS) 1 sc/*dc* into 2nd ch from hook, 1 sc/*dc* into next ch, *sk next 3 chs, F into next ch, sk next 3 chs, 1 sc/*dc* into next ch, **ch 1, sk next ch, 1 sc/*dc* into next ch; rep from * ending last rep at **, 1 sc/*dc* into last ch, turn.
ROW 2: Ch 2, 1 hdc/*htr* into first st, *ch 3, 1 sc/*dc* into ch-1 sp at centre of next fan, ch 3, **V into next sp; rep from * ending last rep at **, 2 hdc/*htr* into last sc/*dc*, turn.

ROW 3: Ch 3, 3 dc/*tr* into first st, *1 sc/*dc* into next ch-3 sp, ch 1, 1 sc/*dc* into next ch-3 sp, **F into centre of next V stitch; rep from * ending last rep at **, 4 dc/*tr* into 2nd of ch-2, turn.
ROW 4: Ch 1, 1 sc/*dc* into first st, *ch 3, V into next sp, ch 3, 1 sc/*dc* into sp at centre of next fan; rep from * ending with 1 sc/*dc* into 3rd of ch-3.
ROW 5: Ch 1, 1 sc/*dc* into first st, *1 sc/*dc* into next ch-3 sp, F into centre of next V stitch, 1 sc/*dc* into next ch-3 sp, **ch 1; rep from * ending last rep at **, 1 sc/*dc* into last sc/*dc*, turn.
Rep Rows 2–5 for length required.
Fasten off yarn.

73 Under the sea

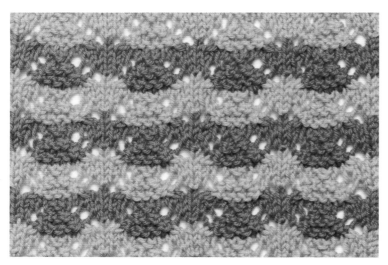

NOTE: Don't break yarn at colour changes, instead carry colour not in use loosely up side of work.

Using yarn A, CO a multiple of 9 sts plus 3.

ROW 1: (RS) K2, *YO, ssk, K4, K2tog, YO, K1; rep from * to last st, K1.

ROW 2: K1, P2, *K6, P3; rep from * to last 9 sts, K6, P2, K1.

ROW 3: K3, *YO, ssk, K2, K2tog, YO, K3; rep from * to end.

ROW 4: K1, P3, *K4, P5; rep from * to last 8 sts, K4, P3, K1.

ROW 5: K4, *YO, ssk, K2tog, YO, K5; rep from * to last 8 sts, YO, ssk, K2tog, YO, K4.

ROW 6: K1, P4, *K2, P7; rep from * to last 7 sts, K2, P4, K1.

Rep Rows 1–6, changing yarns in the following colour sequence: 6 rows in yarn A, 6 rows in yarn B.

Repeat for length required. BO/CO.

74 Bold bobbles

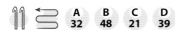

SPECIAL ABBREVIATION:

MB = make bobble (keeping last loop of each stitch on hook, work 4 dc/*tr* into same stitch, YO and draw yarn through all 5 loops).

FOUNDATION CHAIN: Using yarn A, ch 28.

ROW 1: (WS) 1 sc/*dc* into 2nd ch from hook, 1 sc/*dc* into each ch to end, turn. (27 dc/*tr*)

ROW 2: Ch 1, 1 sc/*dc* into each sc/*dc* to end, turn.

ROW 3: Ch 1, 1 sc/*dc* into first sc/*dc*, [MB, 1 sc/*dc* into each of next 2 sc/*dc*] 8 times, MB, 1 sc/*dc* into last sc/*dc*, turn.

ROWS 4 & 5: Rep Row 2.

Rep Rows 2–5 seven times more, changing colours in the following sequence:
4 rows in yarn A, 4 rows in yarn B, 4 rows in yarn C, 4 rows in yarn D, 4 rows in yarn A, 4 rows in yarn B, 4 rows in yarn C, 4 rows in yarn D.

Fasten off yarn.

75 Tiny hearts

CO 33 sts.
Starting at the bottom right-hand corner of the chart, work the 43-row pattern from the chart, reading odd-numbered (RS) rows from right to left and even-numbered (WS) rows from left to right.
BO/CO.

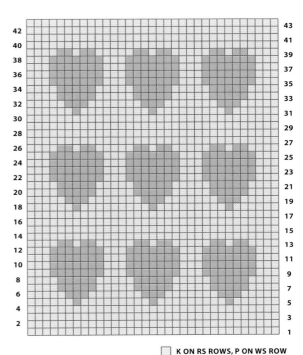

☐ K ON RS ROWS, P ON WS ROW

■ P ON RS ROWS, K ON WS ROWS

76 Jade lattice

FOUNDATION CHAIN: Work a multiple of 6 chains plus 5.

ROW 1: (RS) 1 dc/*tr* into 4th ch from hook, 1 dc/*tr* into each of next 2 chs, *ch 3, sk next 3 chs, 1 dc/*tr* into each of next 3 chs; rep from * to end, turn.

ROW 2: Ch 1, 1 sc/*dc* into each of first 3 dc/*tr*, *ch 3, 1 sc/*dc* into each of next 3 dc/*tr*; rep from * working last sc/*dc* into 3rd of beg skipped ch-3, turn.

ROW 3: Ch 1, 1 sc/*dc* into each of first 3 sc/*dc*, *ch 3, 1 sc/*dc* into each of next 3 sc/*dc*; rep from * to end, turn.

ROW 4: Ch 3 (counts as 1 dc/*tr*), sk first sc/*dc*, 1 dc/*tr* into each of next 2 sc/*dc*, *ch 3, 1 dc/*tr* into each of next 3 sc/*dc*; rep from * to end, turn.

ROW 5: Ch 1, 1 sc/*dc* into each of first 3 dc/*tr*, *ch 3, 1 sc/*dc* into each of next 3 dc/*tr*; rep from * working last sc/*dc* into 3rd of ch-3, turn.

Rep Rows 3–5 for length required. Fasten off yarn.

77 Baby fans

  52

FOUNDATION CHAIN: Work a multiple of 13 chains plus 4.

ROW 1: (RS) 1 dc/*tr* into 4th ch from hook, 1 dc/*tr* into each of next 3 chs, [dc2tog/*tr2tog* over next 2 chs] three times, 1 dc/*tr* into each of next 3 chs, *3 dc/*tr* into next ch, 1 dc/*tr* into each of next 3 chs, [dc2tog/*tr2tog* over next 2 chs] three times, 1 dc/*tr* into each of next 3 chs; rep from * to last ch, 2 dc/*tr* into last ch, turn.

ROW 2: Ch 3, 2 dc/*tr* into first dc/*tr*, ch 2, sk next 3 dc/*tr*, 1 sc/*dc* into next dc/*tr*, ch 4, sk next 3 dc/*tr*, 1 sc/*dc* into next dc/*tr*, ch 2, *sk next 3 dc/*tr*, 5 dc/*tr* into next dc/*tr*, ch 2, sk next 3 dc/*tr*, 1 sc/*dc* in next dc/*tr*, ch 4, sk next 3 dc/*tr*, 1 sc/*dc* into next dc/*tr*, ch 2; rep from * to last 3 dc/*tr*, sk last 3 dc/*tr*, 3 dc/*tr* into beg skipped ch-3, turn.

ROW 3: Ch 3, 1 dc/*tr* into first dc/*tr*, 2 dc/*tr* into next dc/*tr*, 1 dc/*tr* into next dc/*tr*, ch 2, sk next ch-2 sp, 1 sc/*dc* in next ch-4 sp, ch 2, sk next sc/*dc*, 1 dc/*tr* into next dc/*tr*, 2 dc/*tr* into next dc/*tr*, *3 dc/*tr* into next dc/*tr*, 2 dc/*tr* into next dc/*tr*, 1 dc/*tr* into next dc/*tr*, ch 2, sk next ch-2 sp, 1 sc/*dc* into next ch-4 sp, ch 2, sk next sc/*dc*, 1 dc/*tr* into next dc/*tr*, 2 dc/*tr* in next dc/*tr*; rep from * ending rep with 2 dc/*tr* into 3rd of ch-3, turn.

ROW 4: Ch 3, [2 dc/*tr* into next dc/*tr*, 1 dc/*tr* into next dc/*tr*] twice, sk next sc/*dc*, 1 dc/*tr* into next dc/*tr*, *[2 dc/*tr* into next dc/*tr*, 1 dc/*tr* into next dc/*tr*] four times, sk next sc/*dc*, 1 dc/*tr* into next dc/*tr*; rep from * to last 3 dc/*tr*, 2 dc/*tr* into next dc/*tr*, 1 dc/*tr* into next dc/*tr*, 2 dc/*tr* into last dc/*tr*, 1 dc/*tr* into 3rd of ch-3, turn.

ROW 5: Ch 3, 1 dc/*tr* into each of first 4 dc/*tr*, [dc2tog/*tr2tog* over next 2 dc/*tr*] three times, 1 dc/*tr* into each of next 3 dc/*tr*, *3 dc/*tr* in next dc/*tr*, 1 dc/*tr* into each of next 3 dc/*tr*, [dc2tog/*tr2tog* over next 2 dc/*tr*] three times, 1 dc/*tr* into each of next 3 dc/*tr*; rep from * ending rep with 2 dc/*tr* into 3rd of ch-3, turn.

ROW 6: Ch 3, 2 dc/*tr* into first dc/*tr*, ch 2, sk next 3 dc/*tr*, 1 sc/*dc* into next dc/*tr*, ch 4, sk next 3 dc/*tr*, 1 sc/*dc* into next dc/*tr*, ch 2, *sk next 3 dc/*tr*, 5 dc/*tr* into next dc/*tr*, ch 2, sk next 3 dc/*tr*, 1 sc/*dc* into next dc/*tr*, ch 4, sk next 3 dc/*tr*, 1 sc/*dc* into next dc/*tr*, ch 2; rep from * to last 3 dc/*tr*, sk last 3 dc/*tr*, 3 dc/*tr* in 3rd of ch-3, turn.
Rep Rows 3–6 for length required.
Fasten off yarn.

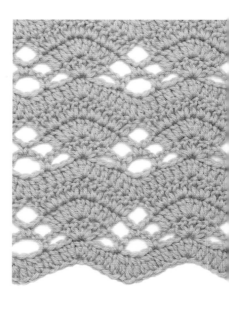

78 Shades of green

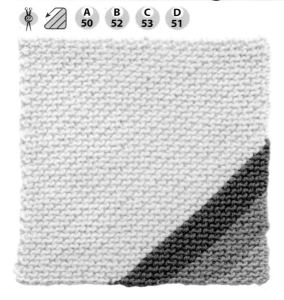 A 50 B 52 C 53 D 51

SPECIAL ABBREVIATION:

INC = increase by knitting into front and back of indicated stitch.

Using yarn A, CO 1 st and inc into it. (2 sts)
Beg increase pattern.
ROW 1: (WS) K1, inc into last st.
ROW 2: K2, inc into last st.
ROW 3: K to last st, inc into last st.
Rep Row 3 until there are 9 sts on needle, ending with a WS row.
Break off yarn A, join yarn B.
Rep Row 3 until there are 17 sts on needle, ending with a WS row.
Break off yarn B, join yarn C.

Rep Row 3 until there are 25 sts on needle, ending with a WS row.
Break off yarn C, join yarn D.
Rep Row 3 until there are 43 sts on needle, ending with a WS row.
K 1 row.
Beg decrease pattern.
ROW 43: K to last 2 sts, K2tog.
Rep Row 43 until 2 sts rem on needle, ending with a WS row.
NEXT ROW: K2tog.
Fasten off yarn.

79 Daisy

| | A 12 | B 10 | C 9 | D 56 | E 52 |

FOUNDATION RING: Using yarn A, ch 6 and join with sl st to form a ring.

ROUND 1: Ch 3 (counts as 1 dc/*tr*), 15 dc/*tr* into ring, join with sl st into 3rd of ch-3. (16 dc/*tr*) Break off yarn A.

ROUND 2: Join yarn B, ch 4 (counts as 1 dc/*tr*, ch 1), [1 dc/*tr* into next dc/*tr*, ch 1] 15 times, join with sl st into 3rd of ch-4. Break off yarn B.

ROUND 3: Join yarn C, ch 3, [2 dc/*tr* into next ch-1 sp, 1 dc/*tr* into next dc/*tr*] 15 times, join with sl st into 3rd of ch-3. (48 dc/*tr*) Break off yarn C.

ROUND 4: Join yarn D, ch 1, 1 sc/*dc* into same place, *ch 5, sl st into 5th ch from hook, sk next 2 dc/*tr*, 1 sc/*dc* into next dc/*tr*, ch 2, sk next 2 dc/*tr*, 1 sc/*dc* into next dc/*tr*, ch 3, sk next 2 dc/*tr*, 1 sc/*dc* into next dc/*tr*, ch 2, sk next 2 dc/*tr*, **1 sc/*dc* into next dc/*tr*; rep from * twice and from * to ** once again, join with sl st into first sc/*dc*.

ROUND 5: Sl st into next ch-5 sp, ch 3, [4 dc/*tr*, ch 3, 5 dc/*tr*] into same sp, *1 sc/*dc* into next ch-2 sp, 5 dc/*tr* into next ch-3 sp, 1 sc/*dc* into next ch-2 sp, **[5 dc/*tr*, ch 3, 5 dc/*tr*] into next ch-5 sp; rep from * twice and from * to ** once more, join with sl st into 3rd of ch-3. Break off yarn D.

ROUND 6: Join yarn E to any corner ch-3 sp, ch 1, [1 sc/*dc*, ch 3, 1 sc/*dc*] into same sp, *ch 5, 1 dc/*tr* in next sc/*dc*, ch 3, sk next 2 dc/*tr*, 1 sc/*dc* into next dc/*tr*, ch 3, sk next 2 dc/*tr*, 1 dc/*tr* into next sc/*dc*, ch 5, **[1 sc/*dc*, ch 3, 1 sc/*dc*] into next ch-3 sp; rep from * twice and from * to ** once again, join with sl st into first sc/*dc*.

ROUND 7: Sl st into next ch-3 sp, ch 3, [2 dc/*tr*, ch 2, 3 dc/*tr*] into same ch-3 sp, *5 dc/*tr* into next ch-5 sp, 3 dc/*tr* into each of next 2 ch-3 sps, 5 dc/*tr* into next ch-5 sp, [3 dc/*tr*, ch 2, 3 dc/*tr*] into next ch-3 sp; rep from * twice and from * to ** once again, join with sl st into 3rd of ch-3.

ROUND 8: Ch 1, 1 sc/*dc* into each dc/*tr* of previous round, working [2 sc/*dc*, ch 2, 2 sc/*dc*] into each ch-2 corner sp, join with sl st into first sc/*dc*.

ROUND 9: Ch 1, 1 sc/*dc* into each sc/*dc* of previous round, working 2 sc/*dc* into each ch-2 corner sp, join with sl st into first sc/*dc*. Fasten off yarn.

80 Coral stripes

| | A 12 | B 51 |

SPECIAL ABBREVIATION:

INC = increase one stitch by lifting horizontal thread between last stitch worked and next stitch and knitting into the back of it.

NOTE: Do not break yarn at colour changes, instead carry yarn not in use loosely up side of work.

Using yarn A, CO a multiple of 13 sts plus 2.

ROW 1: (RS) *K2, inc, K4, sl 1, K2tog, psso, K4, inc; rep from * to last 2 sts, K2.

ROW 2: K1, P to last st, K1.

Rep Rows 1–2, changing yarns in the following colour sequence and ending with a row 2:
2 rows in yarn A,
2 rows in yarn B.
Repeat for length required.
BO/*CO*.

81 Peony

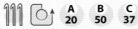

A **B** **C**
20 **50** **37**

FOUNDATION RING: Using yarn A, ch 8 and join with sl st to form a ring.

ROUND 1: Ch 1, 16 sc/*dc* into ring, join with sl st into first sc/*dc*.

ROUND 2: Ch 1, 1 sc/*dc* into same place, [ch 3, sk next sc/*dc*, 1 sc/*dc* into next sc/*dc*] seven times, ch 3, join with sl st into first sc/*dc*.

ROUND 3: Ch 1, 1 sc/*dc* into same place, [ch 5, 1 sc/*dc* into next sc/*dc*] seven times, ch 5, join with sl st into first sc/*dc*.

ROUND 4: Working into ch-3 sps of Round 2 and in front of ch-5 sps of Round 3, sl st into first ch-3 sp, ch 1, *[1 sc/*dc*, ch 1, (1 dc/*tr*, ch 1) five times, 1 sc/*dc*] into same ch-3 sp; rep from * seven times more, join with sl st into first sc/*dc*.

ROUND 5: Ch 1, 1 sc/*dc* into same place, ch 2, *[1 sc/*dc* into next st, ch 2] six times, **1 sc/*dc* into next sc/*dc*, ch 2; rep from * six times and from * to ** once more, join with sl st into first sc/*dc*. Break off yarn A.

ROUND 6: With RS facing, join yarn B to any ch-5 sp of Round 3. Working behind petals, ch 3, 2 dc/*tr* into same ch-5 sp, *[3 tr/*dtr*, ch 2, 3 tr/*dtr*] into next ch-5 sp, **3 dc/*tr* into next ch-5 sp; rep from * twice and from * to ** once more, join with sl st into 3rd of ch-3.

ROUND 7: Ch 3, 1 dc/*tr* into each dc/*tr* and tr/*dtr* of previous round, working [2 dc/*tr*, ch 2, 2 dc/*tr*] into each ch-2 corner sp, join with sl st into 3rd of ch-3.

ROUND 8: Ch 3, 1 dc/*tr* into each dc/*tr* of previous round, working [2 dc/*tr*, ch 2, 2 dc/*tr*] into each ch-2 corner sp, join with sl st into 3rd of ch-3. Break off yarn B.

ROUND 9: Join yarn C and rep Round 8. Break off yarn C.

ROUND 10: Join yarn B. Ch 3, 1 dc/*tr* into each dc/*tr* of previous round, working 5 dc/*tr* into each ch-2 corner sp, join with sl st into 3rd of ch-3.

Fasten off yarn.

82 On the diagonal

  37

CO 1 st.

ROW 1: (WS) K into front, back and front of st. (3 sts)

ROW 2 AND EVERY ALT ROW: K.

ROW 3: K1, YO, K1, YO, K1. (5 sts)

ROW 5: K2, YO, K1, YO, K2. (7 sts)

ROW 7: K3, YO, K1, YO, K3. (9 sts)

Cont working in this way, inc 1 st at either side of centre st of every RS (odd-numbered) row until there are 57 sts on needle, ending with a WS row.
BO/CO.

83 Mint parfait

 A **B**
51 **16**

NOTE: Don't break yarn at colour changes, instead carry colour not in use loosely up side of work.

Using yarn A, CO a multiple of 7 sts plus 2.

ROW 1: K.

ROW 2: K1, P to last st, K1.

ROW 3: K2, *YO, P1, P3tog, P1, YO, K2; rep from * to end.

ROW 4: K1, P to last st, K1.

Rep Rows 1–4, changing yarns in the following colour sequence:
2 rows in yarn A, 2 rows in yarn B.
Repeat for length required.
BO/CO.

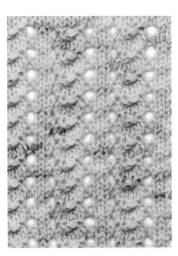

84 Heart quartet

 63

MOTIF SIZE: 13 blocks high by 11 blocks wide.

NOTE: The heart motif can be positioned as required on the mesh background. If repeating the motif, allow at least four spaces between motifs.

WORKING THE MOTIF: Starting at the bottom right-hand corner of the chart, work the blocks and spaces from the chart in filet crochet (see page 121). When following the chart, read odd-numbered (RS) rows from right to left and even-numbered (WS) rows from left to right.
Fasten off yarn.

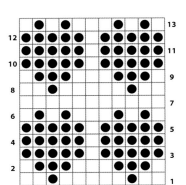

☐ SPACE

● BLOCK

85 Primary ripple

FOUNDATION CHAIN: Using yarn A, work a multiple of 13 chains.

ROW 1: (RS) 1 dc/*tr* into 4th ch from hook, 1 dc/*tr* into each of next 3 chs, *3 dc/*tr* into next ch, 1 dc/*tr* into each of next 5 chs, sk next 2 chs, 1 dc/*tr* into each of next 5 chs, rep from * to last 6 chs, 3 dc/*tr* into next ch, 1 dc/*tr* into each of next 5 chs, turn.

ROW 2: Sl st into 2nd dc/*tr*, ch 3, 1 dc/*tr* into each of next 4 dc/*tr*, *3 dc/*tr* into next dc/*tr*, 1 dc/*tr* into each of next 5 dc/*tr*, sk next 2 dc/*tr*, 1 dc/*tr* into each of next 5 dc/*tr*, rep from * to last 6 sts, 3 dc/*tr* into next dc/*tr*, 1 dc/*tr* into each of next 5 dc/*tr*, turn.

Rep Row 2, changing yarns in the following colour sequence: 2 rows in yarn A, 2 rows in yarn B, 2 rows in yarn C. Repeat for length required. Fasten off yarn.

86 Big stripe

Using yarn A, CO 61 sts and K 1 row.

ROW 1: (RS) Sl 1, K28, sl 1, K2tog, psso, K29.

ROW 2: Sl 1, K to end of row.

ROW 3: Sl 1, K27, sl 1, K2tog, psso, K28.

ROW 4: Sl 1, K to end of row. Cont working in this way, slipping first st on every row and dec 2 sts at centre of every RS (odd-numbered) row until 45 sts rem on needle, ending with a WS row.

Break off yarn A, join yarn B and cont in patt until 5 sts rem on needle, ending with a WS row.

NEXT ROW: Sl 2, K2tog, pass 2nd sl st over K2tog, K1.

NEXT ROW: Sl 1, K2.

NEXT ROW: K3tog. Fasten off yarn.

87 Sunshine

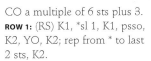

A	B	C
4	49	13

FOUNDATION RING: Using yarn A, ch 6 and join with sl st to form a ring.

ROUND 1: Ch 3 (counts as 1 dc/*tr*), 3 dc/*tr* into ring, ch 3, [4 dc/*tr* into ring, ch 3] three times, join with sl st into 3rd of ch-3.

ROUND 2: Ch 3, *1 dc/*tr* into each of next 3 dc/*tr*, [2 dc/*tr*, ch 3, 2 dc/*tr*] into next ch-3 sp, **1 dc/*tr* into each of next 4 dc/*tr*; rep from * twice and from * to ** once again, join with sl st into 3rd of ch-3.

ROUND 3: Ch 5 (counts as 1 dc/*tr*, ch 2), *1 dc/*tr* into each of next 3 dc/*tr*, [2 dc/*tr*, ch 3, 2 dc/*tr*] into next ch-3 sp, **1 dc/*tr* into each of next 3 dc/*tr*, ch 2; rep from * twice and from * to ** once again, 1 dc/*tr* into each of next 2 dc/*tr*, join with sl st into 3rd of ch-5.

ROUND 4: Ch 5, *1 dc/*tr* into each of next 5 dc/*tr*, [2 dc/*tr*, ch 3, 2 dc/*tr*] into next ch-3 sp, **1 dc/*tr* into each of next 5 dc/*tr*, ch 2; rep from * twice and from * to ** once again, 1 dc/*tr* into each of next 4 dc/*tr*, join with sl st into 3rd of ch-5. Break off yarn A.

ROUND 5: Join yarn B to dc/*tr* before ch-2 sp, ch 5, *1 dc/*tr* into each of next 7 dc/*tr*, [2 dc/*tr*, ch 3, 2 dc/*tr*] into next ch-3 sp, **1 dc/*tr* into each of next 7 dc/*tr*, ch 2; rep from * twice and from * to ** once again, 1 dc/*tr* into each of next 6 dc/*tr*, join with sl st into 3rd of ch-5. Break off yarn B.

ROUND 6: Join yarn C to dc/*tr* before ch-2 sp, ch 5, *1 dc/*tr* into each of next 9 dc/*tr*, [2 dc/*tr*, ch 3, 2 dc/*tr*] into next ch-3 sp, **1 dc/*tr* into each of next 9 dc/*tr*, ch 2; rep from * twice and from * to ** once again, 1 dc/*tr* into each of next 8 dc/*tr*, join with sl st into 3rd of ch-5.

ROUND 7: Ch 1, 1 sc/*dc* into same place, work 1 sc/*dc* into each dc/*tr* of previous round, working 2 sc/*dc* into each ch-2 sp and 3 sc/*dc* into each ch-3 corner sp, join with sl st into first sc/*dc*.
Fasten off yarn.

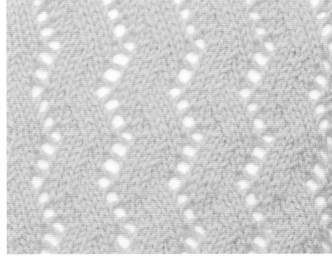

88 Zigzag lace

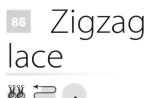

4

CO a multiple of 6 sts plus 3.

ROW 1: (RS) K1, *sl 1, K1, psso, K2, YO, K2; rep from * to last 2 sts, K2.

ROW 2: K1, P to last st, K1.

ROWS 3–6: Rep Rows 1 & 2 twice.

ROW 7: K4, *YO, K2, K2tog, K2; rep from * to last 5 sts, YO, K2, K2tog, K1.

ROW 8: Rep Row 2.

ROWS 9–12: Rep Rows 7 & 8 twice more.
Rep Rows 1–12 for length required.
BO/*CO*.

89 Pavilion

SPECIAL ABBREVIATION:

INC = increase by knitting into front and back of indicated stitch.

NOTE: At colour changes, don't break yarn, instead carry colour not in use loosely up side of work.

Using yarn A, CO 1 st and inc in this st. (2 sts)

Beg increase pattern.

ROW 1: (WS) K1, inc in last st.

ROW 2: K2, inc in last st.

ROW 3: K to last st, inc in last st.

Rep Row 3 until there are 43 sts on needle, ending with a WS row. At the same time, change colours in the following sequence:

2 rows in yarn B, 2 rows in yarn A.

NEXT ROW: Using yarn A, K. Beg decrease pattern.

ROW 43: Using yarn A, K to last 2 sts, K2tog.

Cont to decrease 1 st at end of every row as set until 4 sts rem on needle, ending with a WS row. At the same time, change colours in the following sequence:

2 rows in yarn B, 2 rows in yarn A.

NEXT ROW: Using yarn B, K2, K2tog.

NEXT ROW: K1, K2tog.

NEXT ROW: K2tog.

Fasten off yarn.

90 Block lace

FOUNDATION CHAIN: Work a multiple of 8 chains plus 1.

ROW 1: (RS) 1 dc/*tr* into 7th ch from hook, *ch 1, sk next ch, 1 dc/*tr* into next ch; rep from * to end, turn.

ROW 2: Ch 4 (counts as 1 dc/*tr*, ch 1), sk first dc/*tr*, 1 dc/*tr* into next dc/*tr*, ch 1, *[1 dc/*tr* into next dc/*tr*, 1 dc/*tr* into next ch] twice, [1 dc/*tr* into next dc/*tr*, ch 1] twice; rep from * ending with 1 dc/*tr* into 5th of beg skipped ch-6, turn.

ROW 3: Ch 4, sk first dc/*tr*, 1 dc/*tr* into next dc/*tr*, ch 1, * 1 dc/*tr* into each of next 5 dc/*tr*, ch 1, 1 dc/*tr* into next dc/*tr*, ch 1; rep from * ending with 1 dc/*tr* into 3rd of ch-4, turn.

ROW 4: Ch 4, sk first dc/*tr*, *1 dc/*tr* into next dc/*tr*, ch 1, 1 dc/*tr* into next dc/*tr*, [ch 1, sk next dc/*tr*, 1 dc/*tr* into next dc/*tr*] twice, ch 1; rep from * ending with ch 1, 1 dc/*tr* into next dc/*tr*, ch 1, 1 dc/*tr* into 3rd of ch-4, turn.

ROW 5: Ch 4, sk first dc/*tr*, 1 dc/*tr* into next dc/*tr*, ch 1, *[1 dc/*tr* into next dc/*tr*, 1 dc/*tr* into next ch] twice, [1 dc/*tr* into next dc/*tr*, ch 1] twice; rep from * ending with 1 dc/*tr* into 3rd of ch-4, turn.

Rep Rows 3–5 for length required. Fasten off yarn.

91 Cherries

   A 50 **B 14** **C 56**

BACKGROUND BLOCK

FOUNDATION CHAIN: Using yarn A, ch 29.

ROW 1: (RS) 1 sc/*dc* into 2nd ch from hook, 1 sc/*dc* into each ch to end, turn. (28 sc/*dc*)

ROW 2: Ch 1, 1 sc/*dc* into each sc/*dc* of previous row, turn.
Rep Row 2 32 times more, ending with a WS row.
Fasten off yarn.

CHERRY MOTIFS (MAKE 2)

FOUNDATION RING: Using yarn B, ch 4 and join with sl st to form a ring.

ROUND 1: Ch 3 (counts as 1 dc/*tr*), 15 dc/*tr* into ring, join with sl st into 3rd of ch-3. (16 dc/*tr*)

ROUND 3: Ch 1, 2 sc/*dc* into each dc/*tr* of previous round, join with sl st into first sc/*dc*. (32 sc/*dc*)
Fasten off yarn, leaving a long tail for stitching motifs.
After blocking, pin both cherry motifs to background block using photograph as a guide to placement. Stitch each motif in place with yarn tail. Work stems in couching (see page 116) using yarn C.

92 Waffle

 51

CO a multiple of 3 sts plus 1.

ROW 1: (RS) K1, *K2tog, YO, P1; rep from * to last 3 sts, K2tog, YO, K1.

ROW 2: *K1, P2; rep from * to last st, K1.

ROW 3: K1, YO, sl 1, K1, psso, *P1, YO, sl 1, K1, psso; rep from * to last st, K1.

ROW 4: *K1, P2; rep from * to last st, K1.
Rep Rows 1–4 for length required.
BO/*CO*.

93 Coral seas

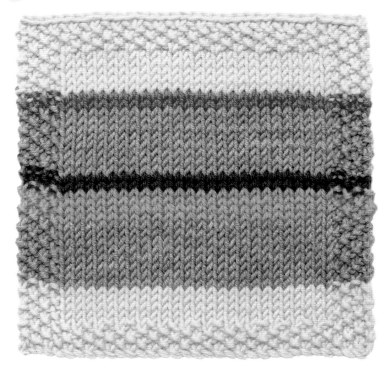

FOUNDATION CHAIN: Using yarn A, work a multiple of 10 chains plus 2.

ROW 1: (RS) 1 sc/*dc* into 2nd ch from hook, 1 sc/*dc* into each ch to end, turn.

ROW 2: Ch 1, sc3tog/*dc3tog*, *1 sc/*dc* into next sc/*dc*, [ch 1, 1 sc/*dc* into next sc/*dc*] four times, sc5tog/*dc5tog*; rep from * to last 8 sc/*dc*, 1 sc/*dc* into next sc/*dc*, [ch 1, 1 sc/*dc* into next sc/*dc*] 4 times, sc3tog/*dc3tog*, turn.

ROW 3: Ch 1, 1 sc/*dc* into each sc/*dc* and ch-1 sp along row, turn.
Rep Rows 2 & 3, changing yarns in the following colour sequence:
2 rows in yarn A, 2 rows in yarn B.
Repeat from * for length required.
Fasten off yarn.

94 Sunset stripes

Using yarn A, CO 33 sts.

ROW 1: (RS) *K1, P1; rep from * to last st, K1.

ROWS 2 , 3 & 4: Rep Row 1.

ROW 5: [K1, P1] twice, K25, [P1, K1] twice.

ROW 6: [K1, P1] twice, P25, [P1, K1] twice.

Rep Rows 5 & 6 16 times more, ending with a Row 6 and changing colours in the following sequence:
8 rows in yarn A, 8 rows in yarn B, 4 rows in yarn C, 2 rows in yarn D, 8 rows in yarn B, 2 rows in yarn E, 6 rows in yarn A.
Cont in yarn A and rep Rows 1–4 once more.
BO/*CO*.

95 Sheringham

 10

CO a multiple of 12 stitches plus 1.

ROWS 1, 3 & 5: (RS) K.

ROW 2: K1, *P1, K2tog, K2, YO, K1, YO, K2, ssk, P1, K1; rep from * to end.

ROW 4: K1, *P1, K2tog, K1, YO, K3, YO, K1, ssk, P1, K1; rep from * to end.

ROW 6: K1, *P1, K2tog, YO, K5, YO, ssk, P1, K1; rep from * to end.

Rep Rows 1–6 for length required. BO/*CO*.

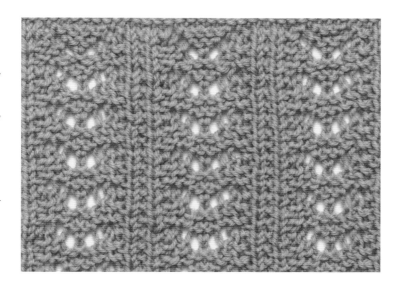

96 Mariner

 A **9** B **12** C **38** D **41**

FOUNDATION RING: Using yarn A, ch 6 and join with sl st to form a ring.

ROUND 1: Ch 3 (counts a 1 dc/*tr*), 15 dc/*tr* into ring, join with sl st into 3rd of ch-3. (16 dc/*tr*)

ROUND 2: Ch 3, 1 dc/*tr* into same place, [2 dc/*tr* into next dc/*tr*] 15 times, join with sl st into 3rd of ch-3. Break off yarn A.

ROUND 3: Join yarn B, ch 3, 2 dc/*tr* into next dc/*tr*, [ch 1, 1 dc/*tr* into next dc/*tr*, 2 dc/*tr* into next dc/*tr*] 15 times, ch 1, join with sl st into 3rd of ch-3. Break off yarn B.

ROUND 4: Join yarn C to any ch-1 sp, *[ch 3, 1 sc/*dc* into next ch-1 sp] three times, ch 6, 1 sc/*dc* into next ch-1 sp; rep from * three times, join with sl st into 3rd of ch-3.

ROUND 5: Ch 3, 2 dc/*tr* into first ch-3 sp, 3 dc/*tr* into each of next 2 ch-3 sps, *[5 dc/*tr*, ch 2, 5 dc/*tr*] into next ch-6 sp, **3 dc/*tr* into each of next 3 ch-3 sps; rep from * twice and from * to ** once more, join with sl st into 3rd of ch-3. Break off yarn C.

ROUND 6: Join yarn D to any dc/*tr* along side of square, ch 3, 1 dc/*tr* into each dc/*tr* of previous round, working [2 dc/*tr*, 1 tr/*dtr*, 2 dc/*tr*] into each ch-2 corner sp, join with sl st into 3rd of ch-3.

ROUND 7: Ch 3, 1 dc/*tr* into each dc/*tr* of previous round, working 5 dc/*tr* into tr/*dtr* at centre of each corner group, join with sl st into 3rd of ch-3.

Fasten off yarn.

97 Flowers

  32

CO 33 sts.
Starting at the bottom right-hand corner of the chart, work the 43-row pattern from the chart, reading odd-numbered (RS) rows from right to left and even-numbered (WS) rows from left to right.
BO/*CO*.

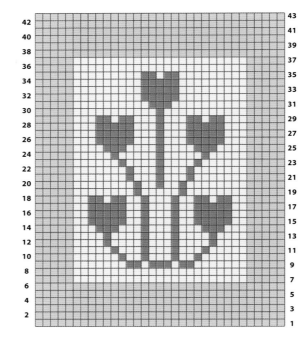

☐ K ON RS ROWS, P ON WS ROWS

▨ K ON BOTH RS AND WS ROWS

■ P ON RS ROWS, K ON WS ROWS

98 Small trellis

  44

FOUNDATION CHAIN: Work a multiple of 3 chains plus 4.
ROW 1: (WS) 1 sc/*dc* into 2nd ch from hook, 1 sc/*dc* into each ch to end, turn.
ROW 2: Ch 4, sk first 2 sc/*dc*, *1 dc/*tr* into each of next 2 sc/*dc*, ch 1, sk next sc/*dc*, 1 sc/*dc* into next sc/*dc*; rep from * to end, turn.

ROW 3: Ch 1, 1 sc/*dc* into each dc/*tr* and ch-1 sp, ending with 1 sc/*dc* into sp made by ch-4 of previous row, 1 sc/*dc* into 3rd of ch-4. Rep Rows 2 & 3 for length required.
Fasten off yarn.

99 Osprey

   A 45 B 46 C 44 D 19

NOTE: Don't break main yarn at colour changes, instead carry it loosely up side of work.

Using yarn A, CO a multiple of 6 sts plus 5.
ROW 1: (RS) [K1, P1] twice, *YO, P3tog, YO, P1, K1, P1; rep from * to last st, K1.
ROW 2: K2, P1, K1, *P3, K1, P1, K1; rep from * to last st, K1.
ROW 3: [K1, P1] twice, *K3, P1, K1, P1; rep from * to last st, K1.
ROW 4: Rep Row 2.
Rep Rows 1–4, changing yarns in the following colour sequence:
6 rows in yarn A, 2 rows in yarn B, 6 rows in yarn A, 2 rows in yarn C, 6 rows in yarn A, 2 rows in yarn D, 6 rows in yarn A, 2 rows in yarn C.
Repeat for length required.
BO/*CO*.

100 Blue dahlia

A 39 **B** 32 **C** 44

FOUNDATION RING: Using yarn A, ch 6 and join with sl st to form a ring.

ROUND 1: Ch 1, [1 sc/*dc*, ch 3, 1 tr/*dtr*, ch 3] into ring eight times, sl st into ring, join with sl st into first sc/*dc*. Break off yarn A.

ROUND 2: Join yarn B into any tr/*dtr*, ch 6, 1 dc/*tr* into fifth ch from hook, ch 1, sk next 2 ch-3 sps, *sl st into next tr/*dtr*, ch 6, 1 dc/*tr* into fifth ch from hook, ch 1, sk next 2 ch-3 sps; rep from *, join with sl st into base of first ch-6. (8 dc/*tr* and 8 ch-4 sps)

ROUND 3: Sl st in next 2 chs and into next ch-4 sp, ch 3 (counts as 1 dc/*tr*), [1 hdc/*htr*, 2 sc/*dc*, ch 2, 2 sc/*dc*, 1 hdc/*htr*, 1 dc/*tr*] into same ch-4 sp, [1 dc/*tr*, 1 hdc/*htr*, 2 sc/*dc*, ch 2, 2 sc/*dc*, 1 hdc/*htr*, 1 dc/*tr*] into each ch-4 sp, join with sl st into 3rd of ch-3. Break off yarn B.

ROUND 4: Join yarn C to any ch-2 sp, ch 1, 1 sc/*dc* into same sp, *ch 2, sk next 2 sc/*dc* and next hdc/*htr*, 1 hdc/*htr* into each of next 2 dc/*tr*, ch 2, 1 sc/*dc* into next ch-2 sp, ch 3, sk next 2 sc/*dc* and next hdc/*htr*, 1 tr/*dtr* into each of next 2 dc/*tr*, ch 3, 1 sc/*dc* into next ch-2 sp; rep from * three times more, omitting last sc/*dc* from final rep, join with sl st into first sc/*dc*.

ROUND 5: Ch 3 (counts as 1 dc/*tr*), *2 dc/*tr* into next ch-2 sp, 1 dc/*tr* into each of next 2 hdc/*htr*, 2 dc/*tr* into next ch-2 sp, 1 dc/*tr* into next sc/*dc*, 3 dc/*tr* into next ch-3 sp, [1 dc/*tr*, 1 tr/*dtr*] into next tr/*dtr*, ch 2, [1 tr/*dtr*, 1 dc/*tr*] into next tr/*dtr*, 3 dc/*tr* into next ch-3 sp, 1 dc/*tr* into next sc/*dc*; rep from * three times more, omitting last dc/*tr* from final rep, join with sl st into 3rd of ch-3.

ROUND 6: Ch 1, 1 sc/*dc* into same place, 1 sc/*dc* into each dc/*tr* and tr/*dtr* of previous round, working 3 sc/*dc* into each ch-2 corner sp, join with sl st into first sc/*dc*. Break off yarn C.

ROUND 7: Join yarn A, ch 3, sk first sc/*dc*, 1 dc/*tr* into each sc/*dc* of previous round, working 3 dc/*tr* into centre st of each 3 sc/*dc* corner group, join with sl st into 3rd of ch-3.

ROUND 8: Ch 1, 1 sc/*dc* into same place, 1 sc/*dc* into each dc/*tr* of previous round, working 3 sc/*dc* into centre st of each 3 dc/*tr* corner group, join with sl st into first sc/*dc*. Fasten off yarn.

101 Baby bells

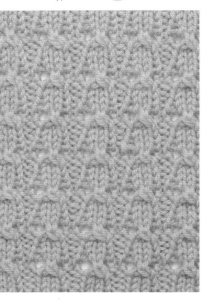

CO a multiple of 5 sts plus 4.
ROWS 1 & 3: (RS) K1, P2, *K3, P2; rep from * to last st, K1.
ROWS 2 & 4: K3, *P3, K2; rep from * to last st, K1.
ROW 5: K1, P2, *YO, sl 1, K2tog, psso, YO, P2; rep from * to last st, K1.
ROW 6: Rep Row 2.
Rep Rows 1–6 for length required.
BO/CO.

102 Eyelet chevrons

FOUNDATION CHAIN: Using yarn A, work a multiple of 10 chains plus 3.
ROW 1: (RS) 1 dc/tr into 4th ch from hook, 1 dc/tr into each of next 3 chs, *sk next 2 chs, 1 dc/tr into each of next 4 chs, ch 2, 1 dc/tr into each of next 4 chs; rep from * to last 6 chs, sk next 2 chs, 1 dc/tr into each of next 3 chs, 2 dc/tr into last ch, turn.
ROW 2: Ch 3 (counts as 1 dc/tr), 1 dc/tr into first dc/tr, 1 dc/tr into each of next 3 dc/tr, *sk next 2 dc/tr, 1 dc/tr into each of next 3 dc/tr, [1 dc/tr, ch 2, 1 dc/tr] into next ch-2 sp, 1 dc/tr into each of next 3 dc/tr; rep from * to last 6 dc/tr, sk next 2 dc/tr, 1 dc/tr into each of next 3 dc/tr, 2 dc/tr into 3rd of beg skipped ch-3, turn.
ROW 3: Ch 3, 1 dc/tr into first dc/tr, 1 dc/tr into each of next 3 dc/tr, *sk next 2 dc/tr, 1 dc/tr into each of next 3 dc/tr, [1 dc/tr, ch 2, 1 dc/tr] into next ch-2 sp, 1 dc/tr into each of next 3 dc/tr; rep from * to last 6 dc/tr, sk next 2 dc/tr, 1 dc/tr into each of next 3 dc/tr, 2 dc/tr into 3rd of ch-3, turn.
Rep Row 3, changing yarns in the following colour sequence: 2 rows in yarn A, 2 rows in yarn B.
Repeat for length required.
Fasten off yarn.

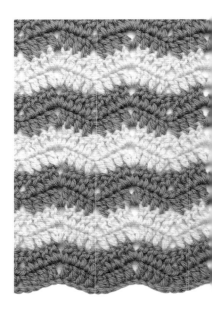

103 African square

SPECIAL ABBREVIATION:

INC = increase by knitting into front and back of indicated stitch.

Using yarn A, CO 1 st, K, P, K into this st and K 1 row.
Beg increase pattern.
ROW 1: (WS) Inc in first st, K to last st, inc in last st.
ROW 2: K.
Rep 2-row inc patt until there are 25 sts on needle, ending with a WS row. Break off yarn A, join yarn B.
Using yarn B, rep 2-row inc patt until there are 31 sts on needle, ending with a WS row.

Break off yarn B, join yarn C.
Using yarn C, rep 2-row inc patt until there are 43 sts on needle, ending with a RS row.
Beg decrease pattern.
NEXT ROW: K2tog tbl, K to last 2 sts, K2tog.
NEXT ROW: K.
Rep 2-row dec patt until 25 sts rem on needle, ending with a WS row.
Break off yarn C, join yarn A.
Using yarn A, rep 2-row dec patt until 3 sts rem on needle, ending with a RS row.
NEXT ROW: K3tog.
Fasten off yarn.

104 Harvest moon

A	B	C	D
1	5	60	57

SPECIAL ABBREVIATIONS:

BEG CL = beginning cluster made from 2 dc/tr sts.

CL = cluster made from 3 dc/tr sts.

FOUNDATION RING: Using yarn A, ch 4 and join with sl st to form a ring.

ROUND 1: Ch 4 (counts as 1 dc/tr, ch 1), [1 dc/tr into ring, ch 1] 11 times, join with sl st into 3rd of ch-4. (12 spaced dc/tr) Break off yarn A.

ROUND 2: Join yarn B to any ch-1 sp, ch 3 (counts as 1 dc/tr), beg CL into first ch-1 sp, [ch 3, CL into next ch-1 sp] 11 times, ch 3, join with sl st into top of beg CL. Break off yarn B.

ROUND 3: Join yarn C to any ch-3 sp, ch 1, 1 sc/dc into same sp, [ch 5, 1 sc/dc into next ch-3 sp] 11 times, ch 5, join with sl st into first sc/dc.

ROUND 4: Sl st into first 3 sts of next ch-5 sp, ch 3, 4 dc/tr into same sp, *ch 1, 1 sc/dc into next ch-5 sp, ch 5, 1 sc/dc into next ch-5 sp, ch 1, **[5 dc/tr, ch 3, 5 dc/tr] into next ch-5 sp; rep from * twice and from * to ** once again, 5 dc/tr into next ch-5 sp, ch 3, join with sl st into 3rd of ch-3. Break off yarn C.

ROUND 5: Join yarn D to any ch-3 sp, ch 3, [1 dc/tr, ch 2, 2 dc/tr] into same sp, *1 dc/tr into each of next 4 dc/tr, ch 4, 1 sc/dc into next ch-5 sp, ch 4, sk next dc/tr, 1 dc/tr into each of next 4 dc/tr, **[2 dc/tr, ch 2, 2 dc/tr] into next ch-3 sp; rep from * twice and from * to ** once again, join with sl st into 3rd of ch-3.

ROUND 6: Sl st into next dc/tr and into next ch-2 sp, ch 3 (counts as 1 dc/tr), [1 dc/tr, ch 2, 2 dc/tr] into same sp, *1 dc/tr into each of next 4 dc/tr, [ch 4, 1 sc/dc into next ch-4 sp] twice, ch 4, sk next 2 dc/tr, 1 dc/tr into each of next 4 dc/tr, **[2 dc/tr, ch 2, 2 dc/tr] into next ch-2 sp; rep from * twice and from * to ** once again, join with sl st into 3rd of ch-3. Break off yarn D.

ROUND 7: Join yarn C to any dc/tr, ch 1, 1 sc/dc into same place, 1 sc/dc into each dc/tr of previous round, working 4 sc/dc into each ch-4 sp along sides and [1 sc/dc, ch 1, 1 sc/dc] into each ch-2 corner sp, join with sl st into first sc/dc.

ROUND 8: Ch 1, 1 sc/dc into same place, 1 sc/dc into each sc/dc of previous round, working 2 sc/dc into each ch-1 corner sp, join with sl st into first dc/tr. Fasten off yarn.

105 Laura's lace

FOUNDATION CHAIN: Work a multiple of 15 chains plus 2.

ROW 1: (RS) 1 dc/*tr* into 4th ch from hook, 1 dc/*tr* into each of next 2 chs, *sk next 3 chs, [1 dc/*tr*, ch 2, 2 dc/*tr*, ch 2, 1 dc/*tr*] into next ch, sk next 3 chs, 1 dc/*tr* into each of next 8 chs; rep from * ending last rep with 4 dc/*tr* into each of last 4 chs, turn.

ROW 2: Ch 5 (counts as 1 dc/*tr*, ch 2), sk first 3 dc/*tr*, 1 dc/*tr* into next dc/*tr*, *ch 2, 1 sc/*dc* into next ch-2 sp, ch 3, 1 sc/*dc* into next ch-2 sp, ch 2, 1 dc/*tr* into next dc/*tr*, ch 2, sk next 2 dc/*tr*, 1 dc/*tr* into each of next 2 dc/*tr*, ch 2, sk next 2 dc/*tr*, 1 dc/*tr* into next dc/*tr*; rep from * to last 4 sts, 1 dc/*tr* into next dc/*tr*, ch 2, sk next 2 dc/*tr*, 1 dc/*tr* into 3rd of beg skipped ch-3, turn.

ROW 3: Ch 3 (counts as 1 dc/*tr*), 2 dc/*tr* into first ch-2 sp, 1 dc/*tr* into next dc/*tr*, *[1 dc/*tr*, ch 2, 2 dc/*tr*, ch 2, 1 dc/*tr*] into next ch-3 sp, 1 dc/*tr* into next dc/*tr*, 2 dc/*tr* into next ch-2 sp, 1 dc/*tr* into each of next 2 dc/*tr*, 2 dc/*tr* into next ch-2 sp, 1 dc/*tr* into next dc/*tr*; rep from * to last dc/*tr*, 1 dc/*tr* into last dc/*tr*, 2 dc/*tr* into sp made by ch-5 of previous row, 1 dc/*tr* into 3rd of ch-5, turn.

ROW 4: Ch 5, sk first 3 dc/*tr*, 1 dc/*tr* into next dc/*tr*, *ch 2, 1 sc/*dc* into next ch-2 sp, ch 3, 1 sc/*dc* into next ch-2 sp, ch 2, 1 dc/*tr* into next dc/*tr*, ch 2, sk next 2 dc/*tr*, 1 dc/*tr* into each of next 2 dc/*tr*, ch 2, sk next 2 dc/*tr*, 1 dc/*tr* into next dc/*tr*; rep from * to last 4 sts, 1 dc/*tr* into next dc/*tr*, ch 2, sk next 2 dc/*tr*, 1 dc/*tr* into 3rd of ch-3, turn.
Rep Rows 3 & 4 for length required. Fasten off yarn.

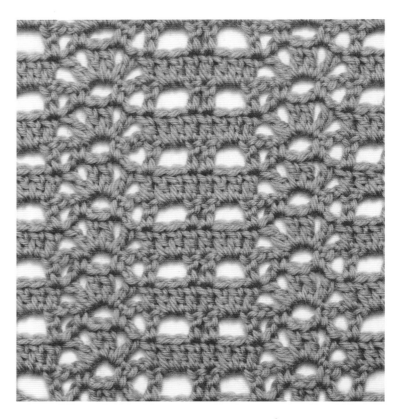

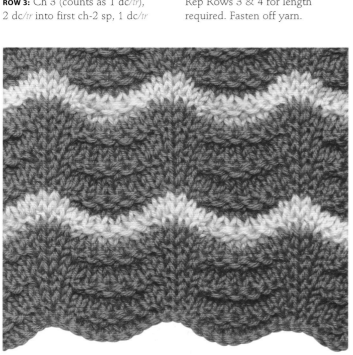

106 Luscious raspberry

SPECIAL ABBREVIATION:

INC = increase one stitch by lifting horizontal thread between last stitch worked and next stitch and knitting into the back of it.

NOTE: At colour changes, don't break main yarn, instead carry it loosely up side of work.

Using yarn A, CO a multiple of 11 sts.

ROW 1: (RS) K.

ROW 2: K1, P to last st, K1.

ROW 3: [P2tog] twice, [inc, K1] three times, inc, *[P2tog] four times, [inc, K1] three times, inc; rep from * to last 4 sts, [P2tog] twice.

ROW 4: K1, P to last st, K1.
Rep Rows 1–4, changing yarns in the following colour sequence:
12 rows in yarn A, 4 rows in yarn B.
Repeat for length required.
BO/*CO*.

107 Happy person

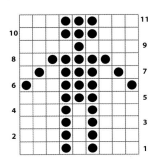

MOTIF SIZE: 11 blocks high by 9 blocks wide.

NOTE: The happy person motif can be positioned as required on the mesh background. If repeating the motif, allow at least four spaces between motifs. To make into a border, arrange motifs so hands overlap.

WORKING THE MOTIF: Starting at the bottom right-hand corner of the chart, work the blocks and spaces from the chart in filet crochet (see page 121). When following the chart, read odd-numbered (RS) rows from right to left and even-numbered (WS) rows from left to right.
Fasten off yarn.

☐ SPACE
● BLOCK

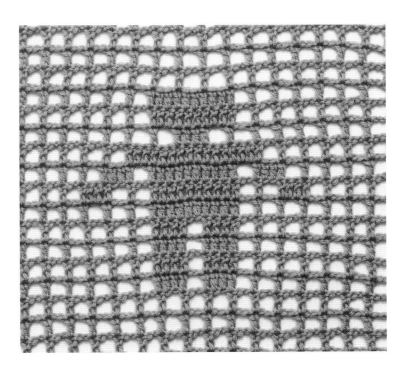

108 Flower show

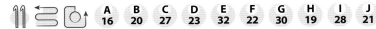

BACKGROUND BLOCK

FOUNDATION CHAIN: Using yarn A, ch 29.

ROW 1: (RS) 1 sc/*dc* into 2nd ch from hook, 1 sc/*dc* into each ch to end, turn. (28 sc/*dc*)

ROW 2: Ch 1, 1 sc/*dc* into each sc/*dc* of previous row, turn.
Rep Row 2 32 times more, ending with a WS row.
Fasten off yarn.

FLOWER MOTIF (MAKE 9)

FOUNDATION RING: Using yarn B, ch 4 and join with sl st into a ring.

ROUND 1: (RS) [Ch 4, 3 tr/*dtr*, ch 4, sl st] into ring four times. Do not join round.
Fasten off yarn, leaving a long yarn tail.
Make one more motif in each remaining colour of yarn. After blocking, pin flowers to background block using photograph as a guide to placement. Stitch each flower securely in place with yarn tail, stitching between petals. If the item is to be washed frequently, work more stitches around outside of petals.

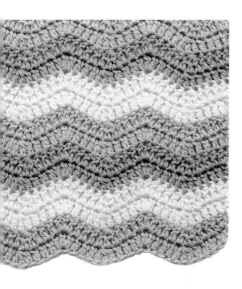

109 Lavender's blue

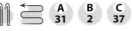 **A 31** **B 2** **C 37**

FOUNDATION CHAIN: Using yarn A, work a multiple of 10 chains plus 3.

ROW 1: (RS) 1 dc/*tr* into 4th ch from hook, 1 dc/*tr* into each of next 3 chs, *dc3tog/*tr3tog*, 1 dc/*tr* into each of next 3 chs, 3 dc/*tr* into next ch, 1 dc/*tr* into each of next 3 chs; rep from * to last ch, 2 dc/*tr* into last ch, turn.

ROW 2: Ch 3, 1 dc/*tr* into same st, 1 dc/*tr* into each of next 3 dc/*tr*, *dc3tog/*tr3tog*, 1 dc/*tr* into each of next 3 dc/*tr*, 3 dc/*tr* into next dc/*tr*, 1 dc/*tr* into each of next 3 dc/*tr*; rep from * to last st, 2 dc/*tr* into 3rd of beg skipped ch-3, turn.

ROW 3: Ch 3, 1 dc/*tr* into same st, 1 dc/*tr* into each of next 3 dc/*tr*, *dc3tog/*tr3tog*, 1 dc/*tr* into each of next 3 dc/*tr*, 3 dc/*tr* into next dc/*tr*, 1 dc/*tr* into each of next 3 dc/*tr*; rep from * to last st, 2 dc/*tr* into 3rd of ch-3, turn.

Rep Row 3, changing yarns in the following colour sequence: 2 rows in yarn A, 2 rows in yarn B, 2 rows in yarn C. Repeat for length required. Fasten off yarn.

110 Diagonal lace

   32

CO 1 st.

ROW 1: (WS) [K1, P1, K1] into same st. (3 sts)

ROW 2: Sl 1, YO, K1, YO, K1.

ROW 3: K.

ROW 4: Sl 1, YO, K3, YO, K1.

ROW 5: K.

Cont working even-numbered (RS) rows as sl 1, YO, K to last 3 sts, YO, K1; and odd-numbered (WS) rows as K, until there are 31 sts on the needle, ending with a WS row.

ROW 30: Sl 1, YO, K1, [YO, K2tog] 14 times, YO, K1.

ROWS 31, 33 & 35: K.

ROW 32: Sl 1, YO, K1, [YO, K2tog] 15 times, YO, K1.

ROW 34: Sl 1, YO, P33, YO, K1.

ROW 36: Sl 1, YO, K35, YO, K1.

ROW 37: P.

ROW 38: Sl 1, YO, K37, YO, K1.

ROW 39: K. (41 sts)

Begin decrease rows.

ROW 40: Sl 1, P2tog, P35, P2tog, P1.

ROW 41: K.

ROW 42: Sl 1, K2tog, K33, K2tog, K1.

ROW 43: P.

ROW 44: Sl 1, K2tog, K31, K2tog, K1.

ROWS 45 & 47: K.

ROW 46: Sl 1, P2tog, P29, P2tog, P1.

ROW 48: Sl 1, K2tog, [YO, K2tog] 14 times, K2tog.

ROW 49: P.

ROW 50: Sl 1, K2tog, [YO, K2tog] 13 times, K2tog.

ROW 51: K.

ROW 52: Sl 1, K2tog, K23, K2tog, K1.

ROW 53: K.

Cont working even-numbered (RS) rows as [sl 1, K2tog, K to last 3 sts, K2tog, K1]; and odd-numbered (WS) rows as K until there are 5 sts on the needle, ending with a WS row.

NEXT ROW: K2tog, K1, K2tog.

NEXT ROW: K3.

NEXT ROW: K3tog.

Fasten off yarn.

111 Violet waves

NOTE: At colour changes, do not break main yarn, instead carry it loosely up side of work.

Using yarn A, CO a multiple of 12 sts plus 1.

ROW 1: (RS) K.

ROWS 2, 3 & 4: Rep Row 1.

ROW 5: K1, *[K2tog] twice, [YO, K1] three times, YO, [sl 1, K1, psso] twice, K1; rep from * to end.

ROW 6: K1, P to last st, K1.

ROWS 7, 9 & 11: Rep Row 5.

ROWS 8 & 10: Rep Row 6.

ROW 12: K1, P to last st, K1. Rep Rows 1–12, changing yarns in the following colour sequence:
4 rows in yarn A, 8 rows in yarn B.
BO/CO.

112 Norfolk lavender

FOUNDATION RING: Using yarn A, ch 6 and join with sl st to form a ring.

ROUND 1: Ch 3 (counts as 1 dc/*tr*), 15 dc/*tr* into ring, join with sl st into 3rd of ch-3. (16 dc/*tr*)

ROUND 2: Ch 3, 1 dc/*tr* into same place, 2 dc/*tr* into each dc/*tr* of previous round, join with sl st into 3rd of ch-3. (32 dc/*tr*) Break off yarn A.

ROUND 3: Join yarn B, ch 3, 1 dc/*tr* into same place, *[1 dc/*tr* into next dc/*tr*, 2 dc/*tr* into next dc/*tr*]; rep from * to last st, 1 dc/*tr* into last st, join with sl st into 3rd of ch-3. (48 dc/*tr*)

ROUND 4: Ch 1, 1 sc/*dc* into same place, *ch 3, sk next 2 dc/*tr*, 1 sc/*dc* into next dc/*tr*; rep from * to last 2 dc/*tr*, ch 3, sk next 2 dc/*tr*, join with sl st into first sc/*dc*. Break off yarn B.

ROUND 5: Join yarn C to any ch-3 sp of previous round, ch 3, [2 dc/*tr*, ch 2, 3 dc/*tr*] into same sp, *1 hdc/*htr*, 2 sc/*dc*] into next ch-3 sp, 3 sc/*dc* into next ch-3 sp, [2 sc/*dc*, 1 hdc/*htr*] into next ch-3 sp, **[3 dc/*tr*, ch 2, 3 dc/*tr*] into next ch-3 sp; rep from * twice and from * to ** once more, join with sl st into 3rd of ch-3.

ROUND 6: Ch 3, 1 dc/*tr* into each of next 2 dc/*tr*, *[2 dc/*tr*, ch 2, 2 dc/*tr*] into next ch-2 corner sp, 1 dc/*tr* into each of next 3 dc/*tr*, 1 dc/*tr* into next hdc/*htr*, 1 dc/*tr* into each of next 7 sc/*dc*, 1 dc/*tr* into next hdc/*htr*, **1 dc/*tr* into each of next 3 dc/*tr*; rep from * twice and from * to ** once more, join with sl st into 3rd of ch-3. Break off yarn C.

ROUND 7: Join yarn A, ch 1, 1 sc/*dc* into each dc/*tr* of previous round, working 3 sc/*dc* into each ch-2 corner sp, join with sl st into first sc/*dc*. Break off yarn A.

ROUND 8: Join yarn B, ch 3, 1 dc/*tr* into each sc/*dc* of previous round, working [2 dc/*tr*, ch 1, 2 dc/*tr*] into centre st of each 3 sc/*dc* corner group, join with sl st into 3rd of ch-3.

ROUND 9: Ch 1, 1 sc/*dc* into each dc/*tr* of previous round, working 2 sc/*dc* into each ch-1 corner sp, join with sl st into first sc/*dc*. Fasten off yarn.

113 Grotto

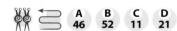

FOUNDATION CHAIN: Work a multiple of 12 chains plus 6.

ROW 1: (WS) 1 dc/*tr* into 6th ch from hook, *sk next 3 chs, 1 sc/*dc* in each of next 5 chs, sk next 3 chs, [1 dc/*tr*, ch 2, 1 dc/*tr*, ch 2, 1 dc/*tr*] in next ch; rep from * ending last rep with [1 dc/*tr*, ch 2, 1 dc/*tr*] in last ch, turn.

ROW 2: Ch 3 (counts as 1 dc/*tr*), 4 dc/*tr* into first ch-2 sp, *sk next dc/*tr* and next sc/*dc*, 1 sc/*dc* into each of next 3 sc/*dc*, 4 dc/*tr* into next ch-2 sp, 1 dc/*tr* into next dc/*tr*, 4 dc/*tr* into next ch-2 sp; rep from * ending with sk next dc/*tr* and next sc/*dc*, 1 sc/*dc* into each of next 3 sc/*dc*, 5 dc/*tr* into sp made by beg skipped ch-5, turn.

ROW 3: Ch 1, 1 sc/*dc* into each of first 3 dc/*tr*, *sk next 2 dc/*tr* and next sc/*dc*, [1 dc/*tr*, ch 2, 1 dc/*tr*, ch 2, 1 dc/*tr*] into next sc/*dc*, sk next sc/*dc* and next 2 dc/*tr*, 1 sc/*dc* into each of next 5 dc/*tr*; rep from * ending with sk next 2 dc/*tr* and next sc/*dc*, [1 dc/*tr*, ch 2, 1 dc/*tr*, ch 2, 1 dc/*tr*] into next sc/*dc*, sk next sc/*dc* and next 2 dc/*tr*, 1 sc/*dc*

into each of next 2 sc/*dc*, 1 sc/*dc* into 3rd of ch-3, turn.

ROW 4: Ch 1, 1 sc/*dc* into first 2 sc/*dc*, *4 dc/*tr* into next ch-2 sp, 1 dc/*tr* into next dc/*tr*, 4 dc/*tr* into next ch-2 sp, sk next sc/*dc*, 1 sc/*dc* into each of next 3 sc/*dc*; rep from * ending last rep with 1 sc/*dc* into each of last 2 sc/*dc*, turn.

ROW 5: Ch 5 (counts as 1 dc/*tr*, ch 2), 1 dc/*tr* into first sc/*dc*, *sk next sc/*dc* and next 2 dc/*tr*, 1 sc/*dc* in each of next 5 dc/*tr*, sk next 2 dc/*tr* and next sc/*dc*, [1 dc/*tr*, ch 2, 1 dc/*tr*, ch 2, 1 dc/*tr*] into next sc/*dc*; rep from * ending last rep with [1 dc/*tr*, ch 2, 1 dc/*tr*] into last sc/*dc*, turn.

ROW 6: Ch 3 (counts as 1 dc/*tr*), 4 dc/*tr* into first ch-2 sp, *sk next dc/*tr* and next sc/*dc*, 1 sc/*dc* in each of next 3 sc/*dc*, 4 dc/*tr* in next ch-2 sp, 1 dc/*tr* in next dc/*tr*, 4 dc/*tr* into next ch-2 sp; rep from * ending with sk next dc/*tr* and next sc/*dc*, 1 sc/*dc* into each of next 3 sc/*dc*, 5 dc/*tr* into sp made by ch-5, turn. Rep Rows 3–6 for length required. Fasten off yarn.

114 Bold chevrons

A	B	C	D
46	52	11	21

SPECIAL ABBREVIATION:

INC = increase by knitting into front and back of indicated stitch.

Using yarn A, CO a multiple of 16 sts plus 2.

ROW 1: (WS) K1, P to last st, K1.

ROW 2: K1, inc in next st, K5, ssk, K2tog, K5, *inc in each of next 2 sts, K5, ssk, K2tog, K5; rep from * to last 2 sts, inc in next st, K1.

Rep Rows 1 & 2, changing yarns in the following colour sequence: 4 rows in yarn A, 2 rows in yarn B, 4 rows in yarn A, 2 rows in yarn C, 4 rows in yarn A, 2 rows in yarn B, 4 rows in yarn A, 2 rows in yarn D. Repeat for length required. BO/*CO*.

115 Blue danube

45

CO 34 sts.

ROW 1: (RS) K.

ROW 2: K1, P to last st, K1.

ROWS 3 & 4: Rep Rows 1 & 2.

ROW 5: K3, *P1, P2tog, YO, K1, YO, P2tog, P1, rep from * to last 3 sts, K3.

ROW 6: Rep Row 2.

ROW 7: Rep Row 1.

ROW 8: K1, P to last st, K1.

Rep Rows 5–8 nine times more, ending with a Row 8.

Rep Row 1 once more.

BO/CO.

116 Pomona

A 24 **B 21** **C 52**

FOUNDATION RING: Using yarn A, ch 4 and join with sl st to form a ring.

ROUND 1: Ch 3 (counts as 1 dc/tr), 11 dc/tr into ring, join with sl st into 3rd of ch-3. (12 dc/tr) Break off yarn A.

ROUND 2: Join yarn B, ch 1, 1 sc/dc into same place, ch 3, 6 sc/dc into 2nd ch from hook, *1 sc/dc into next dc/tr, ch 3, 6 sc/dc into 2nd ch from hook; rep from * 11 times, join with sl st into first sc/dc. Break off yarn B.

ROUND 3: Join yarn C to any sc/dc between petals, ch 1, 1 sc/dc into same place, ch 1, *working behind petals, 1 sc/dc into next sc/dc, ch 1; rep from * 11 times, join with sl st into first sc/dc. (12 sc/dc and 12 ch-1 sps)

ROUND 4: Ch 1, 1 sc/dc into same place, 1 hdc/htr into next ch-1 sp, [1 dc/tr, ch 2, 1 dc/tr] into next sc/dc, 1 hdc/htr into next ch-1 sp, *1 sc/dc into next sc/dc, 1 sc/dc into next ch-1 sp, **1 sc/dc into next sc/dc, 1 hdc/htr into next ch-1 sp, [1 dc/tr, ch 2, 1 dc/tr] into next sc/dc; rep from * twice and from * to ** once more, join with sl st into first sc/dc.

ROUND 5: Ch 3 (counts as 1 dc/tr), 1 dc/tr into each st of previous round, working [2 dc/tr, ch 3, 2 dc/tr] into each ch-2 corner sp, join with sl st into 3rd of ch-3.

ROUND 6: Ch 3, 1 dc/tr into each dc/tr of previous round, working [2 dc/tr, ch 3, 2 dc/tr] into each ch-3 corner sp, join with sl st into 3rd of ch-3.

ROUND 7: Ch 4 (counts as 1 dc/tr, ch 1), [sk next dc/tr, 1 dc/tr in next dc/tr, ch 1] three times, *[1 dc/tr, ch 1, 1 dc/tr, ch 1, 1 dc/tr] in next ch-3 sp, ch 1, 1 dc/tr in next dc/tr, **[ch 1, sk next dc/tr, 1 dc/tr into next dc/tr] seven times; rep from * twice and from * to ** once more, [ch 1, sk next dc/tr, 1 dc/tr in next dc/tr] three times, ch 1, join with sl st into 3rd of ch-4.

ROUND 8: Ch 3, 1 dc/tr into each dc/tr and ch-1 sp of previous round, working [1 dc/tr, ch 3, 1 dc/tr] into centre dc/tr at each corner, join with sl st into 3rd of ch-3. Break off yarn C.

ROUND 9: Join yarn B, ch 1, 1 sc/dc into same place, 1 sc/dc into each dc/tr of previous round, working 5 sc/dc into each ch-3 corner sp, join with sl st into first sc/dc. Fasten off yarn.

117 Ridge & furrow

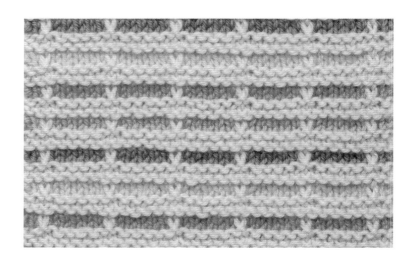

NOTES: Slip all stitches purlwise keeping yarn on wrong side of work. Don't break main yarn at colour changes, instead carry it loosely up side of work.

Using yarn A, CO a multiple of 6 sts plus 5.

ROW 1: (RS) K.

ROWS 2, 3 & 4: Rep Row 1.

ROW 5: K2, *sl 1, K5; rep from * to last 3 sts, sl 1, K2.

ROW 6: K1, P1, sl 1, *P5, sl 1; rep from * to last 2 sts, P1, K1.
Rep Rows 1–6, changing yarns in the following colour sequence:
4 rows in yarn A, 2 rows in yarn B, 4 rows in yarn A, 2 rows in yarn C, 4 rows in yarn A, 2 rows in yarn D, 4 rows in yarn A, 2 rows in yarn E. Repeat for length required. BO/CO.

118 Fancy openwork

NOTE: Either side can be used as RS.

FOUNDATION CHAIN: Work a multiple of 18 chains plus 8.

ROW 1: 1 dc/*tr* into 8th ch from hook, *ch 2, sk next 2 chs, 1 dc/*tr* into next ch; rep from * to end, turn.

ROW 2: Ch 5 (counts as 1 dc/*tr*, ch 2), sk first dc/*tr*, 1 dc/*tr* into next dc/*tr*, *ch 4, 1 tr/*dtr* into each of next 4 dc/*tr*, ch 4, 1 dc/*tr* into next dc/*tr*, ch 2, 1 dc/*tr* into next dc/*tr*; rep from * to end, working last dc/*tr* into 3rd of beg skipped ch-7, turn.

ROW 3: Ch 5, sk first dc/*tr*, 1 dc/*tr* into next dc/*tr*, *ch 4, 1 sc/*dc* into each of next 4 tr/*dtr*, ch 4, 1 dc/*tr* into next dc/*tr*, ch 2, 1 dc/*tr* into next dc/*tr*; rep from * to end, working last dc/*tr* into 3rd of ch-5, turn.

ROWS 4 & 5: Ch 5, sk first dc/*tr*, 1 dc/*tr* into next dc/*tr*, *ch 4, 1 sc/*dc* into each of next 4 sc/*dc*, ch 4, 1 dc/*tr* into next dc/*tr*, ch 2,

1 dc/*tr* into next dc/*tr*; rep from * to end, working last dc/*tr* into 3rd of ch-5, turn.

ROW 6: Ch 5, sk first dc/*tr*, 1 dc/*tr* into next dc/*tr*, *ch 2, [1 tr/*dtr* into next sc/*dc*, ch 2] four times, 1 dc/*tr* into next dc/*tr*, ch 2, 1 dc/*tr* into next dc/*tr*; rep from * to end, working last dc/*tr* into 3rd of ch 5, turn.

ROW 7: Ch 5, sk first dc/*tr*, 1 dc/*tr* into next dc/*tr*, *ch 2, [1 dc/*tr* into next tr/*dtr*, ch 2] four times, 1 dc/*tr* into next dc/*tr*, ch 2, 1 dc/*tr* into next dc/*tr*; rep from * to end, working last dc/*tr* into 3rd of ch-5, turn.

ROW 8: Ch 5, sk first dc/*tr*, 1 dc/*tr* into next dc/*tr*, *ch 4, 1 tr/*dtr* into each of next 4 dc/*tr*, ch 4, 1 dc/*tr* into next dc/*tr*, ch 2, 1 dc/*tr* into next dc/*tr*; rep from * to end, working last dc/*tr* into 3rd of ch-5, turn.
Rep Rows 3–8 for length required. Fasten off yarn.

119 Checkers

  52

CO 33 sts.
Starting at the bottom right-hand corner of the chart, work the 42-row pattern from the chart, reading odd-numbered (RS) rows from right to left and even-numbered (WS) rows from left to right.
BO/CO.

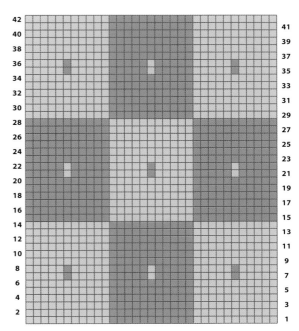

☐ K ON RS ROWS, P ON WS ROWS
☐ P ON RS ROWS, K ON WS ROWS

120 Marigold

 A 3 B 52 C 4

BACKGROUND BLOCK

FOUNDATION CHAIN: Using yarn A, ch 29.

ROW 1: (RS) 1 sc/*dc* into 2nd ch from hook, 1 sc/*dc* into each ch to end, turn. (28 sc/*dc*)

ROW 2: Ch 1, 1 sc/*dc* into each sc/*dc* of previous row, turn.
Rep Row 2 32 times more, ending with a WS row. Fasten off yarn.

LEAF (MAKE 2)

FOUNDATION CHAIN: Using yarn B and leaving a long yarn tail, ch 9.

ROUND 1: Working along one side of ch, 1 sc/*dc* into 2nd ch from hook, 1 sc/*dc* into each of next 6 chs, 4 sc/*dc* into last ch, turn and work back along other side of ch, 1 sc/*dc* into each of next 7 chs. Do not join round.
Fasten off yarn and weave in this end.

FLOWER MOTIF

FOUNDATION RING: Using yarn C, ch 8 and join with sl st into a ring.

ROUND 1: Ch 3 (counts as 1 dc/*tr*), 4 dc/*tr* into ring, ch 3, turn; 1 dc/*tr* into first dc/*tr*, 1 dc/*tr* into each of next 3 dc/*tr*, 1 dc/*tr* into 3rd of ch-3 (petal made), ch 3, turn; *working across back of petal just made, work 5 dc/*tr* into ring, ch 3, turn; 1 dc/*tr* into first dc/*tr*, 1 dc/*tr* into each of next 4 dc/*tr* (petal made), ch 3, turn; rep from * three times more, join round with sl st into 3rd of beg ch-3 of first petal.
Fasten off yarn, leaving a long tail for stitching motif to background.
After blocking, pin leaves and flower to background block using photograph as a guide to placement. Stitch leaves in place with yarn tails, working a row of stitches down centre; stitch flower in place with yarn tail, stitching over the chains beneath each petal.

Pink texture

SPECIAL ABBREVIATION:

CL = cluster made from three single/*double* crochet stitches worked together (sc3tog/*dc3tog*).

FOUNDATION CHAIN: Work a multiple of 2 chains.

ROW 1: (RS) 1 sc/*dc* into 2nd ch from hook, CL inserting hook first into same ch as previous sc/*dc*, then into each of next 2 chs, *ch 1, CL inserting hook first into same ch as 3rd st of previous CL, then into each of next 2 chs; rep from * to end, 1 sc/*dc* into same ch as 3rd st of previous CL, turn.

ROW 2: Ch 1, 1 sc/*dc* into first st, CL inserting hook first into same place as previous sc/*dc*, then into top of next CL, then into next ch-1 sp, *ch 1, CL inserting hook first into same ch-1 sp as 3rd st of previous CL, then into top of next CL, then into next ch-1 sp; rep from * to end working 3rd st of last CL into last sc/*dc*, 1 sc/*dc* into same place, turn.
Rep Row 2 for length required.

Wheatears

CO a multiple of 6 sts plus 5.
ROW 1: (RS) K1, *YO, sl 1, K2tog, psso, YO, K3; rep from * to last 4 sts, YO, sl 1, K2tog, psso, YO, K1.
ROW 2: K1, P to last st, K1.
ROWS 3–8: Rep Rows 1 & 2 three times more.
ROW 9: K4, *YO, sl 1, K2tog, psso, YO, K3; rep from * to last st, K1.
ROW 10: Rep Row 2.
ROWS 11–16: Rep Rows 9 & 10 three times more.
Rep Rows 1–16 for length required.
BO/*CO*.

123 Pretty in pink

FOUNDATION RING: Using yarn A, ch 6 and join with sl st to form a ring.

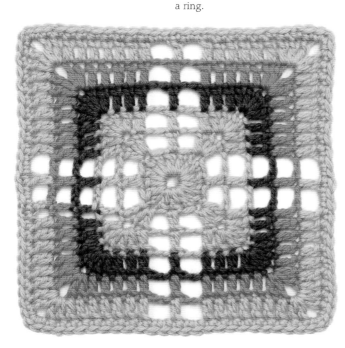

ROUND 1: Ch 3 (counts as 1 dc/*tr*), work 15 dc/*tr* into ring, join with sl st into 3rd of ch-3. (16 dc/*tr*)

ROUND 2: Ch 3, 2 dc/*tr* into same st as sl st, ch 2, sk next dc/*tr*, 1 dc/*tr* into next dc/*tr*, ch 2, sk next dc/*tr*, *3 dc/*tr* into next dc/*tr*, ch 2, sk next dc/*tr*, 1 dc/*tr* into next dc/*tr*, ch 2, sk next dc/*tr*; rep from * twice, join with sl st into 3rd of ch-3.

ROUND 3: Ch 3, 5 dc/*tr* into next dc/*tr*, *1 dc/*tr* into next dc/*tr*, [ch 2, 1 dc/*tr* into next dc/*tr*] twice, 5 dc/*tr* into next dc/*tr*; rep from * twice, [1 dc/*tr* into next dc/*tr*, ch 2] twice, join with sl st into 3rd of ch-3. Break off yarn A.

ROUND 4: Join yarn B. Ch 3, 1 dc/*tr* into each of next 2 dc/*tr*, 5 dc/*tr* into next dc/*tr*, *1 dc/*tr* into each of next 3 dc/*tr*, ch 2, 1 dc/*tr* into next dc/*tr*, ch 2, 1 dc/*tr* into each of next 3 dc/*tr*, 5 dc/*tr* into next dc/*tr*; rep from * twice, 1 dc/*tr* into each of next 3 dc/*tr*, ch 2, 1 dc/*tr* into next dc/*tr*, ch 2, join with sl st into 3rd of ch-3. Break off yarn B.

ROUND 5: Join yarn C. Ch 3, 1 dc/*tr* into each of next 4 dc/*tr*, [2 dc/*tr*, ch 2, 2 dc/*tr*] into next dc/*tr*, *1 dc/*tr* into each of next 5 dc/*tr*, ch 2, 1 dc/*tr* into next dc/*tr*, ch 2, 1 dc/*tr* into each of next 5 dc/*tr*, [2 dc/*tr*, ch 2, 2 dc/*tr*] into next dc/*tr*; rep from * twice, 1 dc/*tr* into each of next 5 dc/*tr*, ch 2, 1 dc/*tr* into next dc/*tr*, ch 2, join with sl st into 3rd of ch-3. Break off yarn C.

ROUND 6: Join yarn A. Ch 3, 1 dc/*tr* in each of next 6 dc/*tr*, [2 dc/*tr*, ch 2, 2 dc/*tr*] into next ch-2 sp, *1 dc/*tr* into each of next 7 dc/*tr*, ch 2, 1 dc/*tr* into next dc/*tr*, ch 2, 1 dc/*tr* into each of next 7 dc/*tr*, [2 dc/*tr*, ch 2, 2 dc/*tr*] into next ch-2 sp; rep from * twice, 1 dc/*tr* into each of next 7 dc/*tr*, ch 2, 1 dc/*tr* into next dc/*tr*, ch 2, join with sl st into 3rd of ch-3.

ROUND 7: Ch 1, 1 sc/*dc* into each dc/*tr* of previous round, working 3 sc/*dc* into each ch-2 corner sp and 2 sc/*dc* into each ch-2 sp along sides of square, join with sl st into first sc/*dc*. Fasten off yarn.

124 Soft triangles

SPECIAL ABBREVIATION:

INC = increase by knitting into front and back of indicated stitch.

Using yarn A, CO 1 st and inc in this st. (2 sts)
Beg increase pattern.
ROW 1: (WS) K1, inc in last st.
ROW 2: K2, inc in last st.
ROW 3: K to last st, inc in last st.

Rep Row 3 until there are 43 sts on needle, ending with a WS row. Break off yarn A, join yarn B and K 1 row.
Beg decrease pattern.
ROW 43: K to last 2 sts, K2tog.
Rep Row 43 until 2 sts rem on needle, ending with a WS row.
NEXT ROW: K2tog.
Fasten off yarn.

125 Butterfly

  68

MOTIF SIZE: 11 blocks high by 13 blocks wide.

NOTE: The butterfly motif can be positioned as required on the mesh background. If repeating the motif, allow at least four spaces between motifs.

WORKING THE MOTIF: Starting at the bottom right-hand corner of the chart, work the blocks and spaces from the chart in filet crochet (see page 121). When following the chart, read odd-numbered (RS) rows from right to left and even-numbered (WS) rows from left to right.
Fasten off yarn.

□ SPACE ● BLOCK

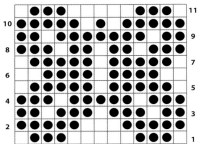

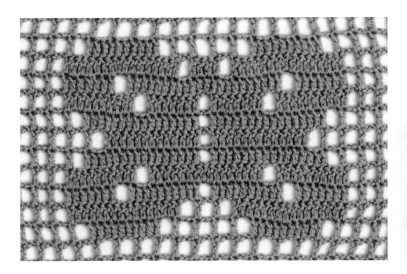

126 Triple strands

   27

NOTE: Either side can be used as RS.

FOUNDATION CHAIN: Work a multiple of 8 chains plus 2.

ROW 1: 1 sc/*dc* into 2nd ch from hook, 1 sc/*dc* into each ch to end, turn.

ROW 2: Ch 1, 1 sc/*dc* into each of first 3 sc/*dc*, *ch 5, sk next 3 sc/*dc*, 1 sc/*dc* into each of next 5 sc/*dc*; rep from * omitting 2 sc/*dc* at end of last rep, turn.

ROW 3: Ch 1, 1 sc/*dc* into each of first 2 sc/*dc*, *ch 3, 1 sc/*dc* into next ch-5 sp, ch 3, sk next sc/*dc*, 1 sc/*dc* into each of next 3 sc/*dc*; rep from * omitting 1 sc/*dc* at end of last rep, turn.

ROW 4: Ch 1, 1 sc/*dc* into first sc/*dc*, *ch 3, 1 sc/*dc* into next ch-3 sp, 1 sc/*dc* into next sc/*dc*, 1 sc/*dc* into next ch-3 sp, ch 3, sk next sc/*dc*, 1 sc/*dc* into next sc/*dc*; rep from * to end, turn.

ROW 5: Ch 5 (counts as 1 dc/*tr*, ch 2), 1 sc/*dc* in next ch-3 sp, 1 sc/*dc* in each of next 3 sc/*dc*, 1 sc/*dc* in next ch-3 sp, *ch 5, 1 sc/*dc* in next ch-3 sp, 1 sc/*dc* in each of next 3 sc/*dc*, 1 sc/*dc* in next ch-3 sp; rep from * to last sc/*dc*, ch 2, 1 dc/*tr* in last sc/*dc*, turn.

ROW 6: Ch 1, 1 sc/*dc* into first dc/*tr*, ch 3, sk next sc/*dc*, 1 sc/*dc* into each of next 3 sc/*dc*, *ch 3, 1 sc/*dc* into next ch-5 sp, ch 3, sk next sc/*dc*, 1 sc/*dc* into each of next 3 sc/*dc*; rep from * to last ch-2 sp, 1 sc/*dc* into 3rd of ch-5, turn.

ROW 7: Ch 1, 1 sc/*dc* into first sc/*dc*, 1 sc/*dc* into next ch-3 sp, ch 3, sk next sc/*dc*, 1 sc/*dc* into next sc/*dc*, *ch 3, 1 sc/*dc* into next ch-3 sp, 1 sc/*dc* into next sc/*dc*, 1 sc/*dc* into next ch-3 sp, ch 3, sk next sc/*dc*, 1 sc/*dc* into next sc/*dc*; rep from * to last ch-3 sp, ch 3, 1 sc/*dc* into ch-3 sp, 1 sc/*dc* into last sc/*dc*, turn.

ROW 8: Ch 1, 1 sc/*dc* into each of first 2 sc/*dc*, *1 sc/*dc* into next ch-3 sp, ch 5, 1 sc/*dc* into next ch-3 sp, 1 sc/*dc* into each of next 3 sc/*dc*; rep from * omitting 1 sc/*dc* at end of last rep, turn.
Rep Rows 3–8 for length required.
Fasten off yarn.

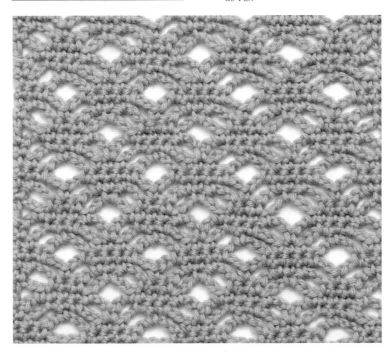

127 Basic block

CO 33 sts.

ROW 1: (RS) *K1, P1; rep from * to last st, K1.

ROWS 2 , 3 & 4: Rep Row 1.

ROW 5: [K1, P1] twice, K25, [P1, K1] twice.

ROW 6: [K1, P1] twice, P25, [P1, K1] twice.

Rep Rows 5 & 6 16 times more, ending with a Row 6.

Rep Rows 1–4 once more.

BO/*CO*.

128 Rosebuds

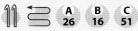

NOTES: When making rosebuds, work foundation chain loosely. Leaf motif is worked around both sides of foundation chain.

BACKGROUND BLOCK

FOUNDATION CHAIN: Using yarn A, ch 29.

ROW 1: (RS) 1 sc/*dc* into 2nd ch from hook, 1 sc/*dc* into each ch to end, turn. (28 sc/*dc*)

ROW 2: Ch 1, 1 sc/*dc* into each sc/*dc* of previous row, turn.

Rep Row 2 32 times more, ending with a WS row.

Fasten off yarn.

ROSEBUD (MAKE 3)

FOUNDATION CHAIN: Using yarn B, ch 20.

ROW 1: (RS) [1 sc/*dc*, ch 3, 1 sc/*dc*] into 2nd ch from hook, *sk next ch, [1 sc/*dc*, ch 3, 1 sc/*dc*] into next ch; rep from * to end.

Fasten off yarn, leaving a long tail. With RS facing and beg with first st, roll up strip tightly to form rosebud. Using long tail, secure base of rosebud by working several stitches through it. Don't cut yarn tail.

LEAF (MAKE 3)

FOUNDATION CHAIN: Using yarn C, ch 7.

ROUND 1: (RS) Working along one side of ch, 1 dc/*tr* into 4th ch from hook, 1 dc/*tr* into next ch, 1 hdc/*htr* into next ch, 3 sc/*dc* into last ch, working along other side of ch, 1 hdc/*htr* into next ch, 1 dc/*tr* into next ch, [1 dc/*tr*, ch 3, sl st] into same ch as first dc/*tr* of round.

Fasten off yarn, leaving a long tail. After blocking, pin rosebuds and leaves to background block using photograph as a guide to placement. Stitch leaves in place with yarn tails, working a row of stitches down centre; stitch rosebuds in place with yarn tail, stitching base securely to background.

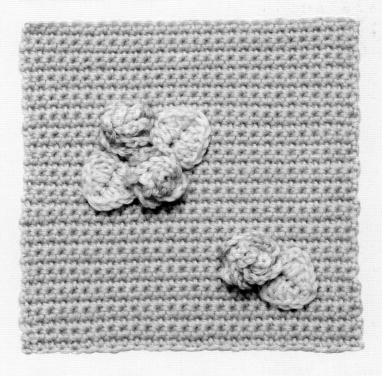

129 Sunday lace

 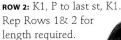 54

CO a multiple of 6 sts plus 5.
ROW 1: (RS) K4, *YO, sl 1, K2tog, psso, YO, K3; rep from * to last st, K1.
ROW 2: K1, P to last st, K1.
Rep Rows 1& 2 for length required.
BO/CO.

130 Evergreen

A 56 · B 54 · C 53 · D 52 · E 50 · F 51

FOUNDATION CHAIN: Using yarn A, ch 6.
ROW 1: (RS) 1 dc/*tr* into 4th ch from hook, 1 dc/*tr* into each of next 2 chs, turn.
ROW 2: Ch 3 (counts as 1 dc/*tr*), 1 dc/*tr* into each of next 2 dc/*tr*, 4 dc/*tr* into loop made by skipped ch-3 of previous row, turn.
ROW 3: Ch 3, 1 dc/*tr* into each of next 2 dc/*tr*, [2 dc/*tr*, ch 2, 2 dc/*tr*] into next dc/*tr*, 1 dc/*tr* into each of next 2 dc/*tr*, 1 dc/*tr* into 3rd of ch-3, turn.
ROW 4: Ch 3, 1 dc/*tr* into each of next 4 dc/*tr*, [2 dc/*tr*, ch 2, 2 dc/*tr*] into ch-2 sp, 1 dc/*tr* into each of next 4 dc/*tr*, 1 dc/*tr* into 3rd of ch-3, turn. Break off yarn A.
ROW 5: Join yarn B, ch 3, 1 dc/*tr* into each of next 6 dc/*tr*, [2 dc/*tr*, ch 2, 2 dc/*tr*] into ch-2 sp, 1 dc/*tr* into each of next 6 dc/*tr*, 1 dc/*tr* into 3rd of ch-3, turn.
ROW 6: Ch 3, 1 dc/*tr* into each of next 8 dc/*tr*, [2 dc/*tr*, ch 2, 2 dc/*tr*] into ch-2 sp, 1 dc/*tr* into each of next 8 dc/*tr*, 1 dc/*tr* into 3rd of ch-3, turn. Break off yarn B.

ROW 7: Join yarn C, ch 3, 1 dc/*tr* into each of next 10 dc/*tr*, [2 dc/*tr*, ch 2, 2 dc/*tr*] into ch-2 sp, 1 dc/*tr* into each of next 10 dc/*tr*, 1 dc/*tr* into 3rd of ch-3, turn.
ROW 8: Ch 3, 1 dc/*tr* into each of next 12 dc/*tr*, [2 dc/*tr*, ch 2, 2 dc/*tr*] into ch-2 sp, 1 dc/*tr* into each of next 12 dc/*tr*, 1 dc/*tr* into 3rd of ch-3, turn. Break off yarn C.
ROW 9: Join yarn D, ch 3, 1 dc/*tr* into each of next 14 dc/*tr*, [2 dc/*tr*, ch 2, 2 dc/*tr*] into ch-2 sp, 1 dc/*tr* into each of next 14 dc/*tr*, 1 dc/*tr* into 3rd of ch-3, turn.
ROW 10: Ch 3, 1 dc/*tr* into each of next 16 dc/*tr*, [2 dc/*tr*, ch 2, 2 dc/*tr*] into ch-2 sp, 1 dc/*tr* into each of next 16 dc/*tr*, 1 dc/*tr* into 3rd of ch-3, turn. Break off yarn D.

ROW 11: Join yarn E, ch 3, 1 dc/*tr* into each of next 18 dc/*tr*, [2 dc/*tr*, ch 2, 2 dc/*tr*] into ch-2 sp, 1 dc/*tr* into each of next 18 dc/*tr*, 1 dc/*tr* into 3rd of ch-3, turn.
ROW 12: Ch 3, 1 dc/*tr* into each of next 20 dc/*tr*, [2 dc/*tr*, ch 2, 2 dc/*tr*] into ch-2 sp, 1 dc/*tr* into each of next 20 dc/*tr*, 1 dc/*tr* into 3rd of ch-3, turn. Break off yarn E.
ROW 13: Join yarn F, ch 3, 1 dc/*tr* into each of next 22 dc/*tr*, [2 dc/*tr*, ch 2, 2 dc/*tr*] into ch-2 sp, 1 dc/*tr* into each of next 22 dc/*tr*, 1 dc/*tr* into 3rd of ch-3, turn.
ROW 14: Ch 3, 1 dc/*tr* into each of next 24 dc/*tr*, 5 dc/*tr* into ch-2 sp, 1 dc/*tr* into each of next 24 dc/*tr*, 1 dc/*tr* into 3rd of ch-3. Fasten off yarn.

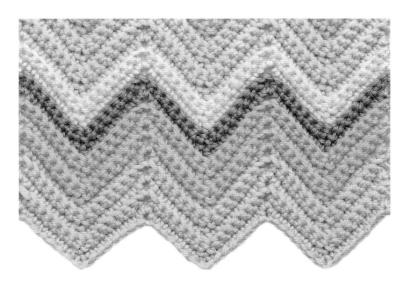

131 Cornrows

| A 50 | B 5 | C 54 | D 3 |

NOTE: After completing Row 1, work into the back loops only of all stitches.

FOUNDATION CHAIN: Using yarn A, work a multiple of 16 chains plus 2.

ROW 1: (RS) 2 sc/*dc* into 2nd ch from hook, *1 sc/*dc* into each of next 7 chs, sk next ch, 1 sc/*dc* into each of next 7 chs, 3 sc/*dc* into next ch; rep from * to end, ending last rep with 2 sc/*dc* into last ch, turn.

ROW 2: Ch 1, 2 sc/*dc* into first sc/*dc*, *1 sc/*dc* into each of next 7 sc/*dc*, sk next 2 sc/*dc*, 1 sc/*dc* into each of next 7 sc/*dc*, 3 sc/*dc* into next sc/*dc*; rep from * to end, ending last rep with 2 sc/*dc* into last sc/*dc*, turn.
Rep Row 2, changing yarns in the following colour sequence:
4 rows in yarn A, 4 rows in yarn B, 2 rows in yarn C, 2 rows in yarn D.
Repeat for length required.
Fasten off yarn.

132 Garden square

  3

SPECIAL ABBREVIATION:

INC = increase by knitting into front and back of indicated stitch.

CO 1 st and inc into it. (2 sts)
Beg increase pattern.
ROW 1: (RS) K1, inc into last st.
ROW 2: K2, inc into last st.
ROW 3: K to last st, inc into last st.
Rep Row 3 until there are 34 sts on needle, ending with a WS row.
ROW 33: K1, P5, *YO, K1, YO, P6; rep from * twice, YO, K1, YO, P5; inc into last st.
ROW 34: K7, *P3 K6; rep from * twice, P3, K5, inc into last st.
ROW 35: K2, P5, *[K1, YO] twice, K1, **P6; rep from * twice and from * to ** once again, P5, K2, inc into last st.
ROW 36: K8, *P5, K6; rep from * three times, inc into last st.
ROW 37: K3, P5, *K2, YO, K1, YO, K2, **P6; rep from * twice and from * to ** once again, P5, K2, inc into last st.

ROW 38: K9, *P7, K6; rep from * twice, P7, K7, inc into last st.
ROW 39: K4, P5, *K3, YO, K1, YO, K3, **P6; rep from * twice and from * to ** once again, P5, K3, inc into last st.
ROW 40: K10, *P9, K6; rep from * twice, P7, K8, inc into last st.
Beg decrease pattern.
ROW 41: K5, P5, *sl 1, K1, psso, K5, K2tog, **P6; rep from * twice and from * to ** once again, P5, K3, K2tog.
ROW 42: K9, *P7, K6; rep from * twice, P7, K8, K2tog.
ROW 43: K4, P5, *sl 1, K1, psso, K3, K2tog, **P6; rep from * twice and from * to ** once again, P5, K2, K2tog.
ROW 44: K8, *P5, K6; rep from * twice, P5, K7, K2tog.
ROW 45: K3, P5, *sl 1, K1, psso, K1, K2tog, **P6; rep from * twice and from * to ** once again, P5, K1, K2tog.

ROW 46: K7, *P3, K6; rep from * twice, P3, K6, K2tog.
ROW 47: K2, P5, *sl 1, K2tog, psso, **P6; rep from * twice and from * to ** once again, P5, K2tog.
ROW 48: K to last 2 sts, K2tog.
Rep Row 48 until 2 sts rem on needle, ending with a WS row.
NEXT ROW: K2tog.
Fasten off yarn.

133 Speckle

A 58 **B** 60 **C** 6 **D** 62

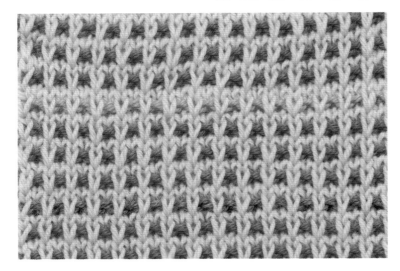

NOTES: Slip all stitches purlwise keeping yarn on wrong side of work. Don't break main yarn at colour changes, instead carry it loosely up side of work.

Using yarn A, CO a multiple of 2 sts plus 1.
ROW 1: (RS) K.
ROW 2: K1, P to last st, K1.
ROW 3: K1, *sl 1, K1; rep from * to end.
ROW 4: K1, *sl 1, K1; rep from * to end.

Rep Rows 1–4, changing yarns in the following colour sequence: 2 rows in yarn A, 2 rows in yarn B, 2 rows in yarn A, 2 rows in yarn B, 2 rows in yarn A, 2 rows in yarn B, 2 rows in yarn A, 2 rows in yarn C, 2 rows in yarn A, 2 rows in yarn B, 2 rows in yarn A, 2 rows in yarn B, 2 rows in yarn A, 2 rows in yarn B, 2 rows in yarn A, 2 rows in yarn D.
Repeat for length required.
BO/CO.

134 Natural stripes

A 58 **B** 59 **C** 8 **D** 60 **E** 61

NOTE: Don't break yarn B at colour changes, instead carry it loosely up side of work.

Using yarn A, CO 33 sts.
ROW 1: (RS) K.
ROW 2: K1, P to last st, K1.

Rep Rows 1 & 2 20 times more, ending with a Row 2 and changing colours in the following sequence: 10 rows in yarn A, 10 rows in yarn B, 2 rows in yarn C, 2 rows in yarn B, 2 rows in yarn D, 4 rows in yarn B, 2 rows in yarn E, 6 rows in yarn B, 4 rows in yarn A.
BO/CO.

135 Russian lace

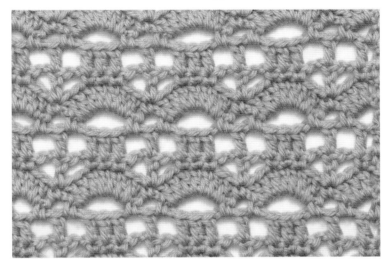

FOUNDATION CHAIN: Work a multiple of 8 chains plus 3.

ROW 1: (RS) 1 dc/*tr* into 4th ch from hook, *ch 2, sk next 2 chs, 1 dc/*tr* into next ch, ch 2, sk next 2 chs, 1 dc/*tr* into each of next 3 chs; rep from * ending last rep with 1 dc/*tr* into each of last 2 chs, turn.

ROW 2: Ch 5, *1 sc/*dc* into next ch-2 sp, ch 3, 1 sc/*dc* into next ch-2 sp, ch 5; rep from * ending last rep with ch 2, 1 dc/*tr* into 3rd of beg skipped ch-3, turn.

ROW 3: Ch 3 (counts as 1 dc/*tr*), 3 dc/*tr* in first ch-2 sp, *1 sc/*dc* into next ch-3 sp, 7 dc/*tr* into next ch-5 sp; rep from * ending last rep with 4 dc/*tr* into sp made by ch-5, turn.

ROW 4: Ch 1, 1 sc/*dc* into each of first 2 dc/*tr*, *ch 2, 1 dc/*tr* into next sc/*dc*, ch 2, sk next 2 dc/*tr*, 1 sc/*dc* into each of next 3 dc/*tr*; rep from * ending last rep with 1 sc/*dc* into last dc/*tr*, 1 sc/*dc* into 3rd of ch-3, turn.

ROW 5: Ch 3, 1 dc/*tr* into 2nd sc/*dc*, *ch 2, 1 dc/*tr* into next dc/*tr*, ch 2, 1 dc/*tr* into each of next 3 sc/*dc*; rep from * ending last rep with 1 dc/*tr* into each of last 2 sc/*dc*, turn.

ROW 6: Ch 5, *1 sc/*dc* into next ch-2 sp, ch 3, 1 sc/*dc* into next ch-2 sp, ch 5; rep from * ending last rep with ch 2, 1 dc/*tr* into 3rd of ch-3, turn.
Rep Rows 3–6 for length required.
Fasten off yarn.

136 Ice flower

FOUNDATION RING: Using yarn A, ch 6 and join with sl st to form a ring.

ROUND 1: Ch 5 (counts as 1 tr/*dtr*, ch 1), [1 tr/*dtr*, ch 1] into ring 15 times, join with sl st into 4th of ch-5. (16 spaced tr/*dtr*) Break off yarn A.

ROUND 2: Join yarn B to any ch-1 sp, 1 sc/*dc* into same sp, [ch 4, sk next ch-1 sp, 1 tr/*dtr* into next ch-1 sp] seven times, ch 4, join with sl st into first sc/*dc*.

ROUND 3: Sl st to first ch-4 sp, ch 4, 4 tr/*dtr* into same sp, [ch 1, 5 tr/*dtr* into next ch-4 sp] seven times, ch 1, join with sl st into 4th of ch-4.
Break off yarn B.

ROUND 4: Join yarn C to any ch-1 sp, 1 sc/*dc* into same sp, ch 4, sk next 2 tr/*dtr*, 1 sc/*dc* into next tr/*dtr*, *ch 4, 1 sc/*dc* into next ch-1 sp, ch 4, sk next 2 tr/*dtr*, 1 sc/*dc* into next tr/*dtr*; rep from * seven times, ch 1, 1 dc/*tr* into first sc/*dc* to make ch-4 sp and join round.

ROUND 5: Ch 1, 1 sc/*dc* into same sp, [ch 4, 1 sc/*dc* into next ch-4 sp] 15 times, ch 4, join with sl st into first sc/*dc*. Break off yarn C.

ROUND 6: Join yarn A to any ch-4 sp, ch 3 (counts as 1 dc/*tr*), [1 dc/*tr*, 2 tr/*dtr*, ch 2, 2 tr/*dtr*, 2 dc/*tr*] into same ch-4 sp, *[2 dc/*tr*, 2 hdc/*htr*] into next ch-4 sp, 4 hdc/*htr* into next ch-4 sp, [2 hdc/*htr*, 2 tr/*dtr*] into next ch-4 sp, **[2 dc/*tr*, 2 tr/*dtr*, ch 2, 2 tr/*dtr*, 2 dc/*tr*] into next ch-4 sp; rep from * twice and from * to ** once more, join with sl st into 3rd of ch-3.

ROUND 7: Ch 3, sk first dc/*tr*, 1 dc/*tr* into each st of previous round, working 5 dc/*tr* into each ch-2 corner sp, join with sl st into 3rd of ch-3.

ROUND 8: Ch 1, 1 sc/*dc* into each dc/*tr* of previous round, working 3 sc/*dc* into centre st of each 5 dc/*tr* corner group, join with sl st into first sc/*dc*.
Fasten off yarn.

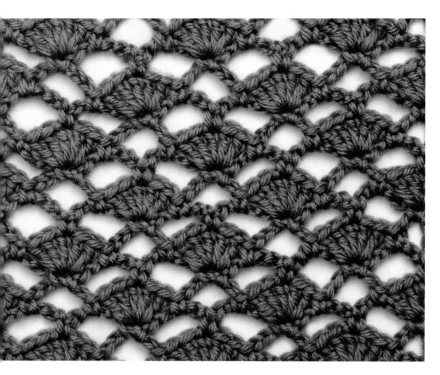

137 Baby trellis

 40

FOUNDATION CHAIN: Work a multiple of 12 chains plus 4.

ROW 1 : (RS) 2 dc/*tr* into 4th ch from hook, *sk next 2 chs, 1 sc/*dc* into next ch, ch 5, sk next 5 chs, 1 sc/*dc* into next ch, sk next 2 chs, 5 dc/*tr* into next ch; rep from * to end, working only 3 dc/*tr* into last ch, turn.

ROW 2: Ch 1, 1 sc/*dc* into first st, *ch 5, 1 sc/*dc* into next ch-5 sp, ch 5, 1 sc/*dc* into 3rd dc/*tr* of next 5 dc/*tr* group; rep from * to end, working last sc/*dc* into 3rd of beg skipped ch-3, turn.

ROW 3: *Ch 5, 1 sc/*dc* into next ch-5 sp, 5 dc/*tr* into next sc/*dc*, 1 sc/*dc* into next ch-5 sp; rep from * ending with ch 2, 1 dc/*tr* into last sc/*dc*, turn.

ROW 4: Ch 1, 1 sc/*dc* into first st, *ch 5, 1 sc/*dc* into 3rd dc/*tr* of next 5 dc/*tr* group, ch 5, 1 sc/*dc* into next ch-5 sp; rep from * to end, turn.

ROW 5: Ch 3, 2 dc/*tr* into first st, *1 sc/*dc* into next ch-5 sp, ch 5, 1 sc/*dc* into next ch-5 sp, 5 dc/*tr* into next sc/*dc*; rep from * to end, working only 3 dc/*tr* into last sc/*dc*, turn.

ROW 6: Ch 1, 1 sc/*dc* into first st, *ch 5, 1 sc/*dc* into next ch-5 sp, ch 5, 1 sc/*dc* into 3rd dc/*tr* of next 5 dc/*tr* group; rep from * to end, working last sc/*dc* into 3rd of ch-3, turn.

Rep Rows 3–6 for length required. Fasten off yarn.

138 Basketweave

 37

CO 35 sts.

ROW 1: (RS) K.

ROWS 2 & 4: K4, P3, *K5, P3; rep from * to last 4 sts, K4.

ROW 3: P4, K3, *P5, K3; rep from * to last 4 sts, P4.

ROW 5: Rep Row 1.

ROW 6: P3, *K5, P3; rep from * to end.

ROW 7: K3, *P5, K3; rep from * to end.

ROW 8: P3, *K5, P3; rep from * to end.

Rep Rows 1–8 five times more, ending with a Row 8.

BO/*CO*.

139 Mini checks

A	B
35	39

NOTES: Slip all stitches purlwise. At colour changes, do not break yarn, but carry colour not in use up side of work.

Using yarn A, CO a multiple of 3 sts.

ROW 1: (RS) K.

ROW 2: K1, P to last st, K1.

ROW 3: K1, sl 1 wyib, *K2, sl 1 wyib; rep from * to last st, K1.

ROW 4: K1, sl 1 wyif, *K2 wyib, sl 1 wyif; rep from * to last st, K1. Rep Rows 1–4, changing yarns in the following colour sequence: 2 rows in yarn A, 2 rows in yarn B.
Repeat for length required.
BO/CO.

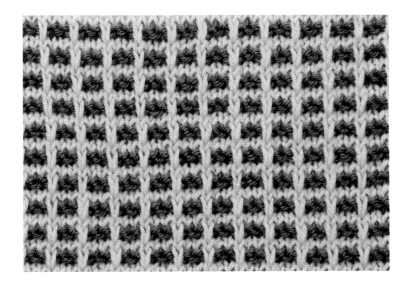

140 Dotty

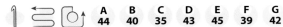

A	B	C	D	E	F	G
44	40	35	43	45	39	42

BACKGROUND BLOCK

FOUNDATION CHAIN: Using yarn A, ch 29.

ROW 1: (RS) 1 sc/*dc* into 2nd ch from hook, 1 sc/*dc* into each ch to end, turn. (28 sc/*dc*)

ROW 2: Ch 1, 1 sc/*dc* into each sc/*dc* of previous row, turn.
Rep Row 2 32 times more, ending with a WS row.
Fasten off yarn.

CIRCULAR MOTIF (MAKE 6)

FOUNDATION RING: Using yarn B, ch 4 and join with sl st to form a ring.

ROUND 1: Ch 3 (counts as 1 dc/*tr*), 15 dc/*tr* into ring, join with sl st into 3rd of ch-3.
Fasten off yarn, leaving a long tail for stitching motif to background. Make one more motif in each remaining colour of yarn. After blocking, pin motifs to background block using photograph as a guide to placement. Stitch each motif in place with yarn tail.

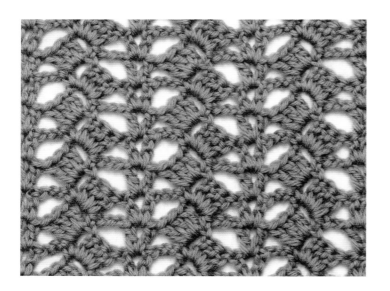

141 Lavender lace

NOTE: Either side can be used as RS.

FOUNDATION CHAIN: Work a multiple of 10 chains plus 4.

ROW 1: 1 dc/*tr* into 4th ch from hook, *ch 3, sk next 4 chs, [1 sc/*dc*, ch 3, 3 dc/*tr*] into next ch, sk next 4 chs, [1 dc/*tr*, ch 1, 1 dc/*tr*] into next ch; rep from * ending last rep with 2 dc/*tr* into last ch, turn.

ROW 2: Ch 3 (counts as 1 dc/*tr*), 1 dc/*tr* into first dc/*tr*, *ch 3, 1 sc/*dc* into 3rd of next ch-3, ch 3, 3 dc/*tr* into sp made by same ch-3 on previous row, [1 dc/*tr*, ch 1, 1 dc/*tr*] into next ch-1 sp; rep from * ending last rep with 2 dc/*tr* into sp made by beg skipped ch-3, turn.

ROW 3: Ch 3, 1 dc/*tr* into first dc/*tr*, *ch 3, 1 sc/*dc* into 3rd of next ch-3, ch 3, 3 dc/*tr* into sp made by same ch-3, [1 dc/*tr*, ch 1, 1 dc/*tr*] into next ch-1 sp; rep from * ending last rep with 2 dc/*tr* into sp made by ch-3, turn.

Rep Row 3 for length required. Fasten off yarn.

142 Mallow

BACKGROUND BLOCK

FOUNDATION CHAIN: Using yarn A, ch 29.

ROW 1: (RS) 1 sc/*dc* into 2nd ch from hook, 1 sc/*dc* into each ch to end, turn. (28 sc/*dc*)

ROW 2: Ch 1, 1 sc/*dc* into each sc/*dc* of previous row, turn.

Rep Row 2 32 times more, ending with a WS row.

Fasten off yarn.

FLOWER MOTIF

FOUNDATION RING: Using yarn B, ch 4 and join with sl st into a ring.

ROUND 1: Ch 5 (counts as 1 dc/*tr*, ch 2), [1 dc/*tr* into ring, ch 2] seven times, join with sl st into 3rd of ch-5.

ROUND 2: Sl st into next ch-2 sp, ch 1, [1 sc/*dc*, 1 hdc/*htr*, 1 dc/*tr*, 1 hdc/*htr*, 1 sc/*dc*] into same sp (petal made), [1 sc/*dc*, 1 hdc/*htr*, 1 dc/*tr*, 1 hdc/*htr*, 1 sc/*dc*] into each rem ch sp, join with sl st into first sc/*dc*.

Break off yarn B.

On the WS, join yarn C to one of the central spokes.

ROUND 3: Using yarn C and working on the WS, ch 6 (counts as 1 dc/*tr*, ch 3), [1 dc/*tr* around next spoke, ch 3] seven times, join with sl st into 3rd of ch-6.

ROUND 4: Ch 1, turn flower to RS, working behind petals of Round 2, [1 sc/*dc*, ch 1, 5 dc/*tr*, ch 1, 1 sc/*dc*] into next ch-3 sp (petal made), [1 sc/*dc*, ch 1, 5 dc/*tr*, ch 1, 1 sc/*dc*] into each rem ch-3 sp, join with sl st to first sc/*dc*.

Fasten off yarn, leaving a long yarn tail.

LEAF MOTIFS (MAKE 3)

FOUNDATION CHAIN: Using yarn C and leaving a long yarn tail at the start, ch 11.

ROUND 1: Working down one side of ch, 1 dc/*tr* into 4th ch from hook, 1 dc/*tr* into each of next 2 chs, 1 hdc/*htr* into each of next 3 chs, 1 sc/*dc* into next ch, 4 sc/*dc* into last ch, working down other side of ch, 1 sc/*dc* into next ch, 1 hdc/*htr* into each of next 3 chs, 1 dc/*tr* into each of next 2 chs, 2 dc/*tr* into last ch.

Fasten off and weave in this end. After blocking, pin motifs to background block using photograph as a guide to placement. Stitch each motif in place with yarn tail, stitching down centre of each leaf and between petals of flower.

143 Linden lea

A	B	C
54	21	32

NOTE: At colour changes, don't break off yarn, but carry colours not in use up side of work.

Using yarn A, CO 61 sts and K 1 row.

ROW 1: (RS) K28, ssk, K1, K2tog, K28.

ROW 2: Using yarn B, K29, P1, K29.

ROW 3: Using yarn C, K27, ssk, K1, K2tog, K27.

ROW 4: Using yarn A, K28, P1, K28.

ROW 5: Using yarn B, K26, ssk, K1, K2tog, K26.

ROW 6: Using yarn C, K27, P1, K27. Cont working in this way, dec 1 st at either side of centre st of every RS (odd-numbered) row and working P1 at the centre of every WS (even-numbered) row.

At the same time, work in colour sequence as set until there are 43 sts on needle, ending with a WS row.

Break off yarns B and C and cont working patt in yarn A until 3 sts rem on needle, ending with a WS row.

NEXT ROW: K3tog.
Fasten off yarn.

144 Single heart

 65

MOTIF SIZE: 13 blocks high by 13 blocks wide.

NOTE: The heart motif can be positioned as required on the mesh background. If repeating the motif, allow at least four spaces between motifs.

WORKING THE MOTIF: Starting at the bottom right-hand corner of the chart, work the blocks and spaces from the chart in filet crochet (see page 121). When following the chart, read odd-numbered (RS) rows from right to left and even-numbered (WS) rows from left to right.
Fasten off yarn.

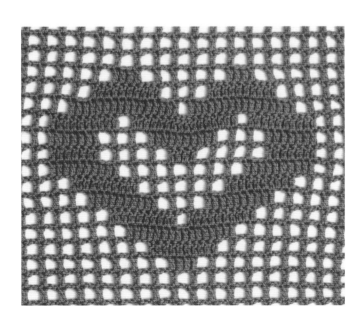

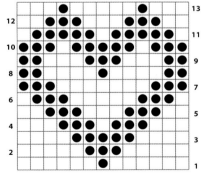

☐ SPACE

● BLOCK

Very green

BLOCK 1

Using yarn A, CO 31 sts and knit 1 row.

ROW 1: (RS) K14, sl 1, K2tog, psso, K14.

ROW 2: K.

ROW 3: K13, sl 1, K2tog, psso, K13.

ROW 4: K.

ROW 5: K12, sl 1, K2tog, psso, K12.

ROW 6: K1, P23, K1.

ROW 7: K11, sl 1, K2tog, psso, K11.

ROW 8: K1, P21, K1.

ROW 9: K10, sl 1 K2tog, psso, K10. Break off yarn A, join yarn B.

ROW 10: K.

Cont working in this way, dec 2 sts at centre of every RS (odd-numbered) row and working WS (even-numbered) rows as K rows until 3 sts rem on needle, ending with a WS row.

NEXT ROW: K3tog. Fasten off yarn.

BLOCK 2

Work as Block 1 using yarn C instead of yarn B.

BLOCK 3

Work as Block 1 using yarn D instead of yarn B.

BLOCK 4

Work as Block 1 using yarn E instead of yarn B.

Using the photograph as a guide to position, stitch the cast-on edges of the four blocks together.

Broken stripes

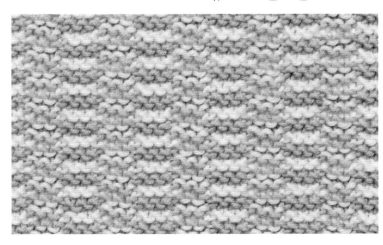

NOTES: Don't break yarn at colour changes, instead carry colour not in use loosely up side of work. Either side can be used as RS.

Using yarn A, CO a multiple of 6 sts plus 3.

ROW 1: *K3, P3; rep from * to last 3 sts, K3.

Rep Row 1, changing yarns in the following colour sequence: 2 rows in yarn A, 2 rows in yarn B.

Repeat for length required.

BO/CO.

147 Bobble tree

SPECIAL ABBREVIATION:

MB = make bobble (keeping last loop of each stitch on hook, work 5 dc/tr into same stitch, YO and draw yarn through all 6 loops).

FOUNDATION CHAIN: Ch 30.

ROW 1: (RS) 1 sc/dc into 2nd ch from hook, 1 sc/dc into each ch to end, turn. (29 dc/tr)

ROW 2: Ch 1, 1 sc/dc into each sc/dc to end, turn.

ROWS 3–7: Rep Row 2.

ROWS 8, 10, 12, 14 & 16: Ch 1, 1 sc/dc into each of next 14 sc/dc, MB, 1 sc/dc into each of next 14 sc/dc, turn.

ROW 9 AND EVERY ALT ROW: Rep Row 2.

ROWS 18 & 22: Ch 1, 1 sc/dc into each of next 10 sc/dc, [MB, 1 sc/dc into next sc/dc] five times, 1 sc/dc into each of next 9 sc/dc, turn.

ROW 20: Ch 1, 1 sc/dc into each of next 9 sc/dc, [MB, 1 sc/dc into next sc/dc] six times, 1 sc/dc into each of next 8 sc/dc, turn.

ROW 24: Ch 1, 1 sc/dc into each of next 11 sc/dc, [MB, 1 sc/dc into next sc/dc] four times, 1 sc/dc into each of next 10 sc/dc, turn.

ROW 26: Ch 1, 1 sc/dc into each of next 12 sc/dc, [MB, 1 sc/dc into next sc/dc] three times, 1 sc/dc into each of next 11 sc/dc, turn.

ROWS 27–32: Rep Row 2.

ROW 33: Ch 1, 1 sc/dc into each sc/dc to end, turn.
Fasten off yarn.

148 Easy shells

  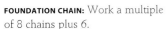

FOUNDATION CHAIN: Work a multiple of 8 chains plus 6.

ROW 1: (RS) 1 dc/tr into 6th ch from hook, *sk next 2 chs, 5 dc/tr into next ch, sk next 2 chs, 1 dc/tr into next ch, ch 1, sk next ch, 1 dc/tr into next ch; rep from * to end, turn.

ROW 2: Ch 4 (counts as 1 dc/tr, ch 1), sk first dc/tr, 1 dc/tr into next dc/tr, *5 dc/tr into centre st of next 5 dc/tr group, sk next 2 dc/tr, 1 dc/tr into next dc/tr, ch 1, 1 dc/tr into next dc/tr; rep from * working last dc/tr into 4th of beg skipped ch-5, turn.

ROW 3: Ch 4, sk first dc/tr, 1 dc/tr into next dc/tr, *5 dc/tr into centre st of next 5 dc/tr group, sk next 2 dc/tr, 1 dc/tr into next dc/tr, ch 1, 1 dc/tr into next dc/tr; rep from * working last dc/tr into 3rd of ch-4, turn.
Rep Row 3 for length required.
Fasten off yarn.

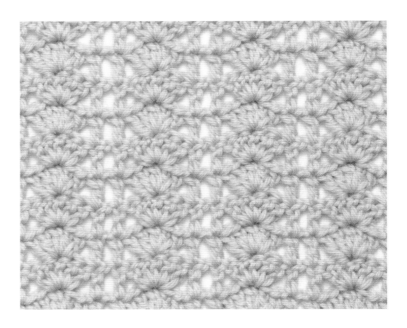

149 Balloons

A 35 B 42 C 49 D 13 E 4

BACKGROUND BLOCK

FOUNDATION CHAIN: Using yarn A, ch 29.

ROW 1: (RS) 1 sc/*dc* into 2nd ch from hook, 1 sc/*dc* into each ch to end, turn. (28 sc/*dc*)

ROW 2: Ch 1, 1 sc/*dc* into each sc/*dc* of previous row, turn.

Rep Row 2 32 times more, ending with a WS row.

Fasten off yarn.

BALLOON MOTIF (MAKE 4)

FOUNDATION RING: Using yarn B, ch 4 and join with sl st to form a ring.

ROUND 1: Ch 3 (counts as 1 dc/*tr*), 15 dc/*tr* into ring, join with sl st into 3rd of ch-3.

Fasten off yarn, leaving a long tail for stitching motif to background. Make one motif in yarns C, D & E. After blocking, pin balloon motifs to background block using photograph as a guide to placement. Stitch each motif in place with yarn tail. Work strings in couching (see page 116) using yarn B.

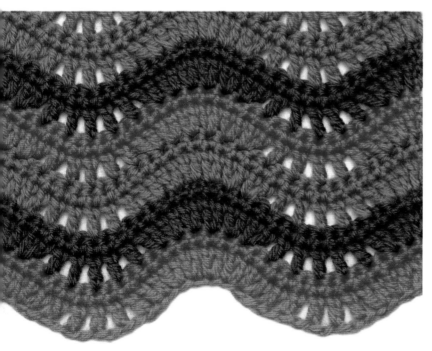

150 Bright waves

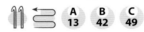

A 13 B 42 C 49

FOUNDATION CHAIN: Work a multiple of 17 chains plus 3.

ROW 1: (RS) 1 dc/*tr* into 4th ch from hook, 2 dc/*tr* into each of next 2 chs, [sk next ch, 1 dc/*tr* into next ch] five times, *sk next ch, 2 dc/*tr* into each of next 6 chs, [sk next ch, 1 dc/*tr* into next ch] five times; rep from * to last 4 chs, sk next ch, 2 dc/*tr* into each of last 3 chs, turn.

ROW 2: Ch 1, 1 sc/*dc* into each dc/*tr* on previous row, 1 sc/*dc* into 3rd of beg skipped ch-3, turn.

ROW 3: Ch 3 (counts as 1 dc/*tr*), 1 dc/*tr* into first sc/*dc*, 2 dc/*tr* into each of next 2 sc/*dc*, [sk next sc/*dc*, 1 dc/*tr* into next sc/*dc*] five times,

*sk next sc/*dc*, 2 dc/*tr* into each of next 6 sc/*dc*, [sk next sc/*dc*, 1 dc/*tr* into next sc/*dc*] five times; rep from * to last 4 sc/*dc*, sk next sc/*dc*, 2 dc/*tr* into each of last 3 sc/*dc*, turn.

ROW 4: Ch 1, 1 sc/*dc* into each dc/*tr* on previous row, 1 sc/*dc* into 3rd of ch-3, turn.

Rep Rows 3 & 4, changing yarns in the following colour sequence: 2 rows in yarn A, 2 rows in yarn B, 2 rows in yarn C.

Repeat for length required.

Fasten off yarn.

151 Citrus triangles

CO a multiple of 5 sts plus 2.

ROW 1: (RS) K.

ROW 2: K1, *K1, P4; rep from * to last st, K1.

ROW 3: K1, *K3, P2; rep from * to last st, K1.

ROW 4: Rep Row 3.

ROW 5: Rep Row 2.

ROW 6: K.

Rep Rows 1–6 for length required.

BO/CO.

152 Big round

A
42

B
4

Using yarn A, CO 33 sts. Starting at the bottom right-hand corner of the chart, work the 42-row pattern from the chart, reading odd-numbered (RS) rows (K all sts) from right to left and even-numbered (WS) rows (P all sts) from left to right.

BO/CO.

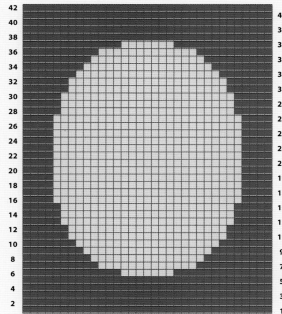

A
B

153 Pastels & cream

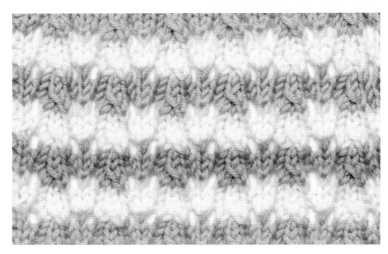

NOTES: At colour changes, don't break yarn B, instead carry it loosely up side of work. Stitch numbers vary, count stitches only after working Row 3.

Using yarn A, CO a multiple of 4 stitches plus 3.
ROW 1: (RS) K2, *YO, K3, YO, K1; rep from * to last st, K1.
ROW 2: K1, P to last st, K1.
ROW 3: K3, sl 1, K2tog, psso, *K3, sl 1, K2tog, psso; rep from * to last 3 sts, K3.

ROW 4: K1, P to last st, K1.
Rep Rows 1–4, changing yarns in the following colour sequence: 4 rows in yarn A, 4 rows in yarn B, 4 rows in yarn C, 4 rows in yarn B, 4 rows in yarn D, 4 rows in yarn B. Repeat for length required. BO/CO.

154 Fern

NOTE: Either side can be used as RS.

FOUNDATION CHAIN: Work a multiple of 8 chains plus 3.
ROW 1: 1 dc/tr into 4th ch from hook, *ch 2, sk next 2 chs, 1 dc/tr into next ch, ch 2, sk next 2 chs, 1 dc/tr into each of next 3 chs; rep from * ending last rep with 1 dc/tr into each of last 2 chs, turn.
ROW 2: Ch 3 (counts as 1 dc/tr), sk first dc/tr, 2 dc/tr into next dc/tr, *ch 1, 1 dc/tr into next dc/tr, ch 1, 2 dc/tr into next dc/tr, 1 dc/tr into next dc/tr, 2 dc/tr into next dc/tr; rep from * ending last rep with 2 dc/tr into last dc/tr, 1 dc/tr into 3rd of beg skipped ch-3, turn.
ROW 3: Ch 3, sk first dc/tr, 1 dc/tr into next dc/tr, 2 dc/tr into next dc/tr, *ch 1, 2 dc/tr into next dc/tr,

1 dc/tr into each of next 3 dc/tr, 2 dc/tr into next dc/tr; rep from * ending last rep with 2 dc/tr into next dc/tr, 1 dc/tr into last dc/tr, 1 dc/tr into 3rd of ch-3, turn.
ROW 4: Ch 3, sk first dc/tr, 1 dc/tr into next dc/tr, *ch 2, 1 dc/tr into next ch-1 sp, ch 2, sk next 2 dc/tr, 1 dc/tr into each of next 3 dc/tr; rep from * ending last rep with ch 2, sk next 2 dc/tr, 1 dc/tr into next dc/tr, 1 dc/tr into 3rd of ch-3, turn.
ROW 5: Ch 3, sk first dc/tr, 2 dc/tr into next dc/tr, *ch 1, 1 dc/tr into next dc/tr, ch 1, 2 dc/tr into next dc/tr, 1 dc/tr into next dc/tr, 2 dc/tr into next dc/tr; rep from * ending last rep with 2 dc/tr into last dc/tr, 1 dc/tr into 3rd of ch-3, turn.
Rep Rows 3–5 for length required. Fasten off yarn.

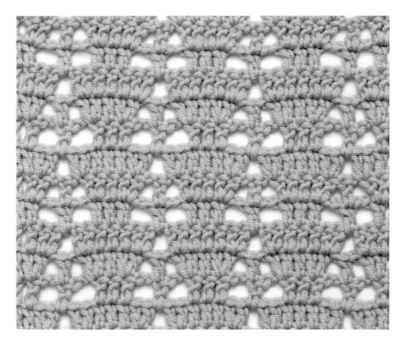

155 Little fish

MOTIF SIZE: 5 blocks high by 7 blocks wide.

NOTE: The fish motif can be positioned as required on the mesh background. If repeating the motif, allow at least four spaces between motifs.

WORKING THE MOTIF: Starting at the bottom right-hand corner of the chart, work the blocks and spaces from the chart in filet crochet (see page 121). When following the chart, read odd-numbered (RS) rows from right to left and even-numbered (WS) rows from left to right.

Fasten off yarn.

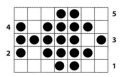

☐ SPACE

● BLOCK

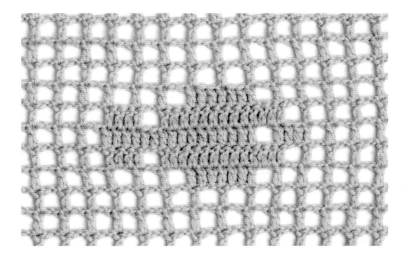

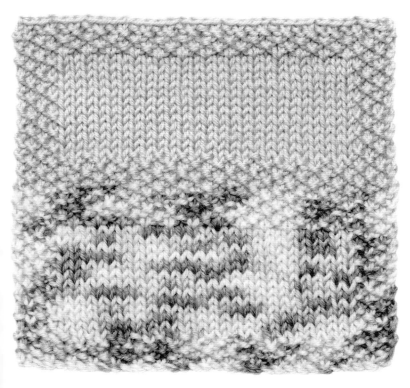

156 Half & half

Using yarn A, CO 33 sts.

ROW 1: (RS) *K1, P1; rep from * to last st, K1.

ROWS 2, 3 & 4: Rep Row 1.

ROW 5: [K1, P1] twice, K25, [P1, K1] twice.

ROW 6: [K1, P1] twice, P25, [P1, K1] twice.

Rep Rows 5 & 6 five times more, ending with a Row 6.

NEXT ROW: Rep Row 5.

Rep Rows 1–4 once more.

Break off yarn A, join yarn B.

Using yarn B, rep Rows 1–4.

NEXT ROW: Rep Row 1.

Rep Rows 5 & 6 six times more, ending with a Row 6.

Rep Rows 1–4 once more.

BO/CO.

157 Patch

Using yarn A, CO 33 sts.
Starting at the bottom right-hand corner of the chart, work the 42-row pattern from the chart, reading odd-numbered (RS) rows (K all sts) from right to left and even-numbered (WS) rows (P all sts) from left to right. BO/CO.

After blocking, work straight stitches in yarn C at right angles to the edges of the patch, arranging the stitches unevenly and making them of varying lengths.

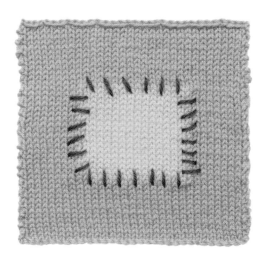

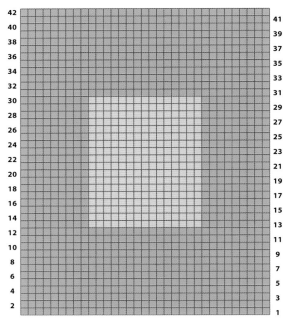

■ A
□ B

158 Buttercup

SPECIAL ABBREVIATION:

MB = make bobble (keeping last loop of each stitch on hook, work 5 dc/tr into same stitch, YO and draw yarn through all 6 loops).

FOUNDATION CHAIN: Ch 30.
ROW 1: (RS) 1 sc into 2nd ch from hook, 1 sc into each ch to end, turn. (29 dc/tr)
ROW 2: Ch 1, 1 sc/dc into each sc/dc to end, turn.
ROWS 3–9: Rep Row 2.
ROW 10: Ch 1, 1 sc/dc into each of next 13 sc/dc, [MB, 1 sc/dc into next sc/dc] twice, 1 sc/dc into each of next 12 sc/dc, turn.

ROW 11 AND EVERY ALT ROW: Rep row 2.
ROW 12: Ch 1, 1 sc/dc into each of next 12 sc/dc, [MB, 1 sc/dc into each of next 3 sc/dc] twice, 1 sc/dc into each of next 9 sc/dc, turn.
ROW 14: Ch 1, 1 sc into each of next 8 sc, *[MB, 1 sc/dc into next sc/dc] twice, 1 sc/dc into next sc/dc; rep from * once more, 1 sc/dc into each of next 12 sc/dc, turn.
ROW 16: Ch 1, 1 sc/dc into each of next 7 sc/dc, [MB, 1 sc/dc into each of next 3 sc/dc] twice, 1 sc/dc into each of next 3 sc/dc, [MB, 1 sc/dc into next sc/dc] twice, 1 sc/dc into each of next 7 sc/dc, turn.

ROW 18: Ch 1, 1 sc/dc into each of next 8 sc/dc, *[MB, 1 sc/dc into next sc/dc] twice, 1 sc/dc into each of next 5 sc/dc, [MB, 1 sc/dc into each of next 3 sc/dc] twice, 1 sc/dc into each of next 4 sc/dc, turn.
ROW 20: Ch 1, 1 sc/dc into each of next 13 sc/dc, *[MB, 1 sc/dc into next sc/dc] twice, 1 sc/dc into next sc/dc; rep from * once more, 1 sc/dc into each of next 7 sc/dc, turn.
ROW 22: Rep Row 12.
ROW 24: Rep Row 10.
ROWS 25–32: Rep Row 2.
ROW 33: Ch 1, 1 sc/dc into each sc/dc to end, turn.
Fasten off yarn.

159 Woven bands

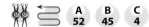

NOTES: Slip all stitches purlwise keeping yarn on wrong side of work. Don't break main yarn at colour changes, instead carry it loosely up side of work.

Using yarn A, CO a multiple of 6 sts plus 3.

ROW 1: (RS) K.

ROW 2: K1, P to last st, K1.

ROW 3: K4, *sl 1, K5; rep from * to last 5 sts, sl 1, K4.

ROW 4: Rep Row 3.

ROW 5: K1, P3, *sl 1, P5; rep from * to last 5 sts, sl 1, P3, K1.

ROW 6: Rep Row 3.

ROWS 7 & 8: Rep Rows 1 & 2.

ROW 9: K1, *sl 1, K5; rep from * to last 2 sts, sl 1, K1.

ROW 10: Rep Row 9.

ROW 11: K1, *sl 1, P5; rep from * to last 2 sts, sl 1, K1.

ROW 12: Rep Row 9.

Rep Rows 1–12, changing yarns in the following colour sequence: 2 rows in yarn A, 4 rows in yarn B, 2 rows in yarn A, 4 rows in yarn C.

Repeat for length required.

BO/CO.

160 Caspian

FOUNDATION CHAIN: Work a multiple of 10 chains plus 2.

ROW 1: (RS) 1 dc/*tr* into 4th ch from hook, *sk next ch, 4 dc/*tr* into next ch, ch 2, 1 dc/*tr* into same ch as 4 dc/*tr*, sk next 3 chs, 1 dc/*tr* into each of next 5 chs; rep from * ending last rep with 1 dc/*tr* into each of last 2 dc/*tr*, turn.

ROW 2: Ch 3, 1 dc/*tr* into 2nd dc/*tr*, *4 dc/*tr* into next ch-2 sp, ch 2, 1 dc/*tr* into same ch-2 sp as 4 dc/*tr*, 1 dc/*tr* into each of next 5 dc/*tr*; rep from * ending last rep with 1 dc/*tr* into last dc/*tr*, 1 dc/*tr* into 3rd of beg skipped ch-3, turn.

ROW 3: Ch 3, 1 dc/*tr* into 2nd dc/*tr*, *4 dc/*tr* into next ch-2 sp, ch 2, 1 dc/*tr* into same ch-2 sp as 4 dc/*tr*, 1 dc/*tr* into each of next 5 dc/*tr*; rep from * ending last rep with 1 dc/*tr* into last dc/*tr*, 1 dc/*tr* into 3rd of ch-3, turn.

Rep Row 3 for length required.

Fasten off yarn.

161 Straight edging

  20

CO 11 sts.
ROW 1: (RS) K2, P2, K1, YO, K2tog,
P2, K2.
ROW 2: K4, P3, K4.
ROW 3: K.
ROW 4: K2, P7, K2.
Rep Rows 1–4 for length required.
BO/CO.

162 Faux ribbing

  19

FOUNDATION CHAIN: Ch 9.
ROW 1: (RS) 1 sc/*dc* into 2nd ch
from hook, 1 sc/*dc* into each ch
to end, turn.
ROW 2: Ch 1, working into back
loops only, 1 sc/*dc* into each st
along row, turn.

Rep Row 2 for length required.
Fasten off yarn.

163 Bias strip

  16

SPECIAL ABBREVIATION:

INC = *increase by knitting into the
front and back of indicated stitch.*

CO 9 sts.
ROW 1: (RS) Inc in first st, K6,
K2tog.
ROW 2: K1, P7, K1.
Rep Rows 1 & 2 for length
required.
BO/CO.

164 Narrow braid

FOUNDATION RING: Ch 4 and join with sl st to form a ring.
ROW 1: (RS) Ch 3 (counts as 1 dc/*tr*), [3 dc/*tr*, ch 2, 4 dc/*tr*] into ring, turn.
ROW 2: Ch 3, [3 dc/*tr*, ch 2, 3 dc/*tr*] into ch-2 sp, 1 dc/*tr* into top of turning chain, turn.
Rep Row 2 for length required. Fasten off yarn.

165 Tiny trimming

SPECIAL ABBREVIATION:
INC = increase by knitting into the front and back of indicated stitch.

CO 5 sts.
ROW 1: (WS) K1, YO, K1, YO, K2tog, inc in last st.

ROW 2: BO/*CO* 2 sts, P3, K1.
Rep Rows 1 & 2 for length required.
BO/*CO*.

166 Belgian lace

FOUNDATION CHAIN: Ch 10.
ROW 1: (RS) 1 dc/*tr* into 7th ch from hook, 1 dc/*tr* into each ch to end, turn. (4 dc/*tr*)
ROW 2: Ch 6, 1 dc/*tr* into each dc/*tr* of previous row, turn.
Rep Row 2 for length required. Fasten off yarn.

167 Puff lace edging

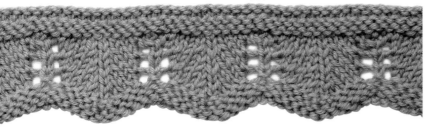

CO a multiple of 11 sts plus 2.
ROWS 1 & 3: (WS) K1, P to last st, K1.
ROWS 2 & 4: K.
ROW 5: K1, *K2tog, K3, YO, K1, YO, K3, K2tog; rep from * to last st, K1.

ROW 6: K1, P to last st, K1.
Rep Rows 5 & 6 three times more, ending with a Row 6.
P 1 row, K 2 rows.
BO/CO.

168 Zigzag edging

CO 8 sts and K 1 row.
ROW 1: (WS) Sl 1, K1, [YO, K2tog] twice, YO, K2.
ROWS 2, 4, 6 & 8: Sl 1, K to end of row.
ROW 3: Sl 1, K2, [YO, K2tog] twice, YO, K2.
ROW 5: Sl 1, K3, [YO, K2tog] twice, YO, K2.

ROW 7: Sl 1, K4, [YO, K2tog] twice, YO, K2.
ROW 9: Sl 1, K11.
ROW 10: BO/CO 4 sts, K to end of row.
Rep Rows 1–10 for length required.
BO/CO.

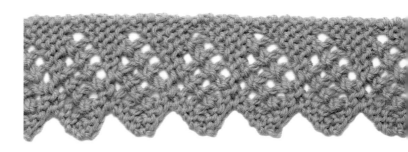

169 Trellis edging

CO 13 sts.
ROW 1 AND EVERY ALT ROW: (WS) K2, P to last 2 sts, K2.
ROW 2: K7, YO, sl 1, K1, psso, YO, K4.
ROW 4: K6, [YO, sl 1, K1, psso] twice, YO, K4.
ROW 6: K5, [YO, sl 1, K1, psso] three times, YO, K4.
ROW 8: K4, [YO, sl 1, K1, psso] four times, YO, K4.
ROW 10: K3, [YO, sl 1, K1, psso] five times, YO, K4.

ROW 12: K4, [YO, sl 1, K1, psso] five times, K2tog, K2.
ROW 14: K5, [YO, sl 1, K1, psso] four times, K2tog, K2.
ROW 16: K6, [YO, sl 1, K1, psso] three times, K2tog, K2.
ROW 18: K7, [YO, sl 1, K1, psso] twice, K2tog, K2.
ROW 20: K8, YO, sl 1, K1, psso, K2tog, K2.
Rep Rows 1–20 for length required.
BO/CO.

170 Little shell edging

FOUNDATION CHAIN: Work a multiple of 4 chains plus 2.
ROW 1: (RS) 1 sc/*dc* into 2nd ch from hook, 1 sc/*dc* into each ch to end, turn.
ROW 2: Ch 1, 1 sc/*dc* into first sc/*dc* and into each sc/*dc* to end, turn.

ROW 3: Ch 1, 1 sc/*dc* into first sc/*dc*, *sk next sc/*dc*, 5 dc/*tr* into next sc/*dc*, sk next sc/*dc*, 1 sc/*dc* into next sc/*dc*; rep from * to end. Fasten off yarn.

171 Shell & lattice edging

FOUNDATION CHAIN: Work a multiple of 6 chains plus 3.
ROW 1 (RS): 1 sc/*dc* into 2nd ch from hook, 1 sc/*dc* into each ch to end, turn.
ROW 2: Ch 1, 1 sc/*dc* into first sc/*dc* and into each sc/*dc* to end, turn.
ROW 3: Ch 3, sk first sc/*dc*, 1 dc/*tr* into next sc/*dc*, *ch 1, sk next sc/*dc*, 1 dc/*tr* into each of next 2 sc/*dc*; rep from * to end, turn.

ROW 4: Ch 5, 1 sc/*dc* into next ch-1 sp, *ch 4, 1 sc/*dc* into next ch-1 sp; rep from * to last 2 sts, ch 2, 1 dc/*tr* into 3rd of ch-3, turn.
ROW 5: Ch 1, 1 sc/*dc* into first dc/*tr*, *7 dc/*tr* into next ch-4 sp, 1 sc/*dc* into next ch-4 sp; rep from * to end, working last sc/*dc* into 3rd of ch-5.
Fasten off yarn.

172 Deep mesh edging

FOUNDATION CHAIN: Ch 20.
ROW 1: (RS) 1 dc/*tr* into 4th ch from hook, 1 dc/*tr* into each of next 2 chs, *ch 1, sk next ch, 1 dc/*tr* into next ch; rep from * to end, turn.
ROW 2: Ch 7, 1 dc/*tr* into first dc/*tr*, [ch 1, 1 dc/*tr* into next dc/*tr*] seven times, 1 dc/*tr* into each of next 2 dc/*tr*, 1 dc/*tr* into 3rd of beg skipped ch-3, turn.

ROW 3: Ch 3, 1 dc/*tr* into each of next 3 dc/*tr*, *ch 1, 1 dc/*tr* into next dc/*tr*; rep from * to end, turn.
ROW 4: Ch 7, 1 dc/*tr* into first dc/*tr*, [ch 1, 1 dc/*tr* into next dc/*tr*] seven times, 1 dc/*tr* into each of next 2 dc/*tr*, 1 dc/*tr* into 3rd of ch-3, turn.
Rep Rows 3 & 4 for length required.
Fasten off yarn.

173 Narrow ruffled edging

CO 12 sts.
ROW 1: (WS) K.
ROW 2: P9, turn, K9.
ROW 3: P9, K3.
ROW 4: K3, P9.
ROW 5: K9, turn, P9.
ROW 6: K.
Rep Rows 1–6 for length required.
BO/*CO*.

174 Shetland lace edging

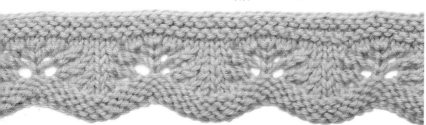

CO a multiple of 11 sts plus 2.
ROWS 1 & 3: (RS) K1, P to last st, K1.
ROW 2: K.
ROWS 4, 6, 8 & 10: Rep Row 1.

ROWS 5, 7 & 9: K1, *[K2tog] twice, [YO, K1] three times, YO, [K2tog] twice; rep from * to last st, K1.
ROWS 11, 12, 13 & 14: K.
BO/*CO*.

175 Fan edging

FOUNDATION CHAIN: Work a multiple of 10 chains plus 7.
ROW 1: (RS) 1 dc/*tr* into 4th ch from hook, 1 dc/*tr* into each ch to end, turn.
ROW 2: Ch 1, 1 sc/*dc* into each of next 5 dc/*tr*, *sk next 2 dc/*tr*, 7 dc/*tr* into next dc/*tr*, sk next 2 dc/*tr*, 1 sc/*dc* into each of next 5 dc/*tr*; rep from * to last 4 dc/*tr*, 1 sc/*dc* into each of last 4 dc/*tr*, 1 sc/*dc* into 3rd of beg skipped ch-3, turn.
ROW 3: Ch 1, 1 sc/*dc* into each of next 4 sc/*dc*, *sk next sc/*dc*, ch 1, [1 dc/*tr* into next dc/*tr*, ch 1] seven times, sk next sc/*dc*, 1 sc/*dc* into each of next 3 sc/*dc*; rep from * to last sc/*dc*, 1 sc/*dc* into last sc/*dc*, turn.
ROW 4: Ch 1, 1 sc/*dc* into each of next 3 sc/*dc*, *ch 1, [1 dc/*tr* into next dc/*tr*, ch 2] six times, 1 dc/*tr* into next dc/*tr*, ch 1, sk next sc/*dc*, 1 sc/*dc* into next sc/*dc*; rep from * to last 2 sc/*dc*, 1 sc/*dc* into each of last 2 sc/*dc*.
Fasten off yarn.

176 Block edging

 45

FOUNDATION CHAIN: Work a multiple of 4 chains plus 1.
ROW 1: (RS) 1 sc/*dc* into 2nd ch from hook, 1 sc/*dc* into each ch to end, turn.
ROW 2: Ch 1, 1 sc/*dc* into each sc/*dc* of previous row, turn.

ROW 3: Ch 3, sk next 2 sc/*dc*, 1 dc/*tr* into next sc/*dc*, *ch 3, 4 dc/*tr* into sp made by dc/*tr* just worked, sk next 3 sc/*dc*, 1 dc/*tr* into next sc/*dc*; rep from * to end.
Fasten off yarn.

177 Fringed edging

   21

CO 20 sts.
ROW 1: (RS) BO/*CO* 15 sts, K4.
ROW 2: K5.
ROW 3: CO 15 sts.
Rep Rows 1–3 for length required.
BO/*CO*.

178 Scallop edging

  32

FOUNDATION CHAIN: Ch 5.
ROW 1: (WS) [3 dc/*tr*, ch 3, 3 dc/*tr*] into 5th ch from hook, turn.
ROWS 2 & 3: Ch 3, [3 dc/*tr*, ch 3, 3 dc/*tr*] into ch-3 sp, turn.
ROW 4: Ch 5, [3 dc/*tr*, ch 3, 3 dc/*tr*] into ch-3 sp, turn.
ROW 5: Ch 3, [3 dc/*tr*, ch 3, 3 dc/*tr*] into ch-3 sp, ch 2, [1 dc/*tr* into ch-5 sp, ch 2] five times, [1 dc/*tr*, 1 sc/*dc*] into next ch-3 sp, turn, ch 3, 2 dc/*tr* into next ch-2 sp, *sl st into next ch-2 sp, ch 3, 2 dc/*tr* into same sp; rep from * three times, 1 sc/*dc* into next ch-2 sp, ch 3, [3 dc/*tr*, ch 3, 3 dc/*tr*] into next ch-3 sp, turn.

ROW 6: Ch 3, [3 dc/*tr*, ch 3, 3 dc/*tr*] into ch-3 sp, turn.
ROW 7: Ch 5, [3 dc/*tr*, ch 3, 3 dc/*tr*] into ch-3 sp, turn.
Rep Rows 5–7 for length required, ending with a Row 4, omitting instructions after working 1 sc/*dc* into ch-2 sp.
Do not break yarn.
Turn edging so RS is facing, scallops are along bottom edge and beg working across top of edging.
NEXT ROW: *Ch 3, 3 sc/*dc* into next ch-3 sp; rep from * to end, working last 3 sc/*dc* into top of beg ch-5, turn.

NEXT ROW: Ch 1, 1 sc/*dc* into each sc/*dc* of previous row, working 3 sc/*dc* into each ch-3 sp, turn.
NEXT ROW: Ch 1, 1 sc/*dc* into each sc/*dc* of previous row.
Fasten off yarn.

179 Sawtooth edging

 🧶 **39**

CO 8 sts and K 1 row.

ROW 1: (WS) Sl 1, K1, [YO, K2tog] twice, YO, K2.

ROW 2: K2, YO, K2, [YO, K2tog] twice, K1.

ROW 3: Sl 1, K1, [YO, K2tog] twice, K2, YO, K2.

ROW 4: K2, YO, K4, [YO, K2tog] twice, K1.

ROW 5: Sl 1, K1, [YO, K2tog] twice, K4, YO, K2.

ROW 6: K2, YO, K6, [YO, K2tog] twice, K1.

ROW 7: Sl 1, K1, [YO, K2tog] twice, K6, YO, K2.

ROW 8: K2, YO, K8, [YO, K2tog] twice, K1.

ROW 9: Sl 1, K1, [YO, K2tog] twice, K8, YO, K2.

ROW 10: K2, YO, K10, [YO, K2tog] twice, K1.

ROW 11: Sl 1, K1, [YO, K2tog] twice, K10, YO, K2.

ROW 12: BO/CO 11 sts, K2, [YO, K2tog] twice, K1.

Rep Rows 1–12 for length required.

BO/CO.

180 Vandyke petal edging

 🧶 **37**

FOUNDATION CHAIN: Ch 23.

ROW 1: (WS) 1 dc/tr into 8th ch from hook, sk next 2 chs, [1 dc/tr, ch 2, 1 dc/tr] into next ch, sk next 2 chs, 1 dc/tr into next ch, ch 2, sk next 2 chs, 1 dc/tr into next ch, ch 5, sk next 5 chs, [1 dc/tr, ch 3, 1 dc/tr] into last ch, turn.

ROW 2: Ch 3 (counts as 1 dc/tr), 7 dc/tr into ch-3 sp, 1 dc/tr into next dc/tr, 7 dc/tr into ch-5 sp, 1 dc/tr into next dc/tr, ch 2, sk 2 chs, 1 dc/tr into next dc/tr, [1 dc/tr, ch 2, 1 dc/tr] into next sp, sk 1 dc/tr, 1 dc/tr into next dc/tr, ch 2, sk 2 chs, 1 dc/tr into next ch, turn.

ROW 3: Ch 5, 1 dc/tr into first dc/tr, [1 dc/tr, ch 2, 1 dc/tr] into next ch-2 sp, sk 1 dc/tr, 1 dc/tr into next dc/tr, ch 2, sk 2 chs, 1 dc/tr into next dc/tr, ch 5, sk next 7 dc/tr, [1 dc/tr, ch 3, 1 dc/tr] into next dc/tr, turn.

Repeat Rows 2 & 3 for length required.

Fasten off yarn.

181 Lacy garter edging

 🧶 **45**

CO 15 sts.

ROW 1: (WS) K11, YO, K2tog, YO, K2.

ROWS 2, 4 & 6: K.

ROW 3: K12, YO, K2tog, YO, K2.

ROW 5: K13, YO, K2tog, YO, K2.

ROW 7: K14, YO, K2tog, YO, K2.

ROW 8: BO/CO 4 sts, K to end.

Rep Rows 1–8 for length required.

BO/CO.

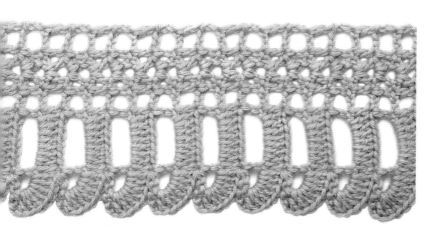

182 Ridged edging

 40

CO 6 sts.
ROWS 1, 2 & 3: K.
ROW 4: CO 3 sts, K to end.
ROWS 5, 6 & 7: Rep Row 1.
ROW 8: CO 3 sts, K to end.
ROWS 9, 11, 13, 14 & 15: Rep Row 1.
ROWS 10 & 12: P.
ROW 16: BO/CO 3 sts, K to end.
ROWS 17, 18 & 19: Rep Row 1.

ROW 20: BO/CO 3 sts, K to end.
Rep Rows 1–20 for length required.
BO/CO.

183 Century edging

 44

FOUNDATION CHAIN: Work a multiple of 11 chains plus 7.
ROW 1: (RS) 1 sc/*dc* into 2nd ch from hook, 1 sc/*dc* into each ch to end, turn.
ROW 2: Ch 1, 1 sc/*dc* into first sc/*dc*, ch 5, sk next 4 sc/*dc*, 1 sc/*dc* into next sc/*dc*, *ch 9, sl st into 6th ch from hook, ch 3, sk next 5 sc/*dc*, 1 sc/*dc* into next sc/*dc*, ch 5,

sk next 4 sc/*dc*, 1 sc/*dc* into next sc/*dc*; rep from * to end, turn.
ROW 3: Ch 1, 2 sc/*dc* into next ch-5 sp, *ch 1, [3 dc/*tr*, ch 3] three times into next ch-6 sp, 3 dc/*tr* into same ch-6 sp, ch 1, 2 sc/*dc* into next ch-5 sp; rep from * to end.
Fasten off yarn.

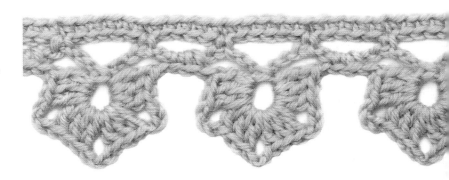

184 Baby picot edging

 38

SPECIAL ABBREVIATION:
MP = make picot by working [ch 4, sl st into 4th ch from hook].

FOUNDATION CHAIN: Work a multiple of 5 chains plus 2.
ROW 1: (WS) 1 sc/*dc* into 2nd ch from hook, 1 sc/*dc* into each ch to end, turn.

ROW 2: Ch 3, [1 dc/*tr*, MP, 2 dc/*tr*] into first sc/*dc*, *sk next 4 sc/*dc*, [2 dc/*tr*, MP, 2 dc/*tr*] into next sc/*dc*; rep from * to end.
Fasten off yarn.

185 Pointed edging

  51

CO 6 sts.

ROWS 1, 3, 5 & 7: (RS) Sl 1, K1, YO, K2tog, YO, K to end.

ROWS 2, 4 & 6: Sl 1, K to last 3 sts, YO, K2tog, K1.

ROW 8: BO/CO 4 sts, K2, YO, K2tog, K1.
Rep Rows 1–8 for length required.
BO/CO.

186 Shell braid

 52

FOUNDATION CHAIN: Ch 3.

ROW 1: (RS) [3 dc/*tr*, ch 3, 3 dc/*tr*] into 3rd ch from hook, turn.

ROW 2: Ch 3, [3 dc/*tr*, ch 3, 3 dc/*tr*] into ch-3 sp of previous row, turn. Rep Row 2 for length required. Fasten off yarn.

187 Shamrock edging

 52

FOUNDATION CHAIN: Ch 9.

ROW 1: (WS) 1 dc/*tr* into 4th ch from hook, 1 dc/*tr* into each of next 2 chs, ch 2, sk next 2 chs, [1 dc/*tr* into last ch, ch 2] three times, 1 dc/*tr* into same ch, turn.

ROW 2: Ch 1, [1 sc/*dc*, 2 dc/*tr*, 1 sc/*dc*] into first ch-2 sp, [1 sc/*dc*, 3 dc/*tr*, ch 2, 3 dc/*tr*, 1 sc/*dc*] into next ch-2 sp, [1 sc/*dc*, 2 dc/*tr*, 1 sc/*dc*] into next ch-2 sp, ch 2, 1 dc/*tr* into each of next 3 dc/*tr*, 1 dc/*tr* into top of turning ch, turn.

ROW 3: Ch 3 (counts as 1 dc/*tr*), 1 dc/*tr* into each of next 3 dc/*tr*, ch 2, [1 dc/*tr*, ch 2 into next ch-2 sp] three times, 1 dc/*tr* into same sp, turn. Rep Rows 2 & 3 for length required. Fasten off yarn.

188 Pretty edging

  54

FOUNDATION CHAIN: Work a multiple of 8 chains plus 2.

ROW 1: (WS) 1 sc/*dc* into 2nd ch from hook, 1 sc/*dc* into each ch to end, turn.

ROW 2: Ch 1, 1 sc/*dc* into next sc/*dc*, *ch 3, sk next 3 sc/*dc*, 3 dc/*tr* into next sc/*dc*, turn; ch 5, sk next 2 dc/*tr*, sl st into next dc/*tr*, turn; ch 1, 7 sc/*dc* into next ch-5 sp, ch 3, sk next 3 sc/*dc*, 1 sc/*dc* into next sc/*dc*; rep from * to end. Fasten off yarn.

189 Narrow leaves

 49

SPECIAL ABBREVIATION:

INC = increase by knitting into the front, back and front of indicated stitch.

CO 7 sts.
ROW 1: (RS) K.
ROW 2: K3, P1, K3.
ROW 3: K2, P1, inc into next st, P1, K2.
ROW 4: K3, P3, K3.
ROW 5: K2, P1, [K1, YO] twice, K1, P1, K2.
ROW 6: K3, P5, K3.
ROW 7: K2, P1, K2, YO, K1, YO, K2, P1, K2.

ROW 8: K3, P7, K3.
ROW 9: K2, P1, K3, YO, K1, YO, K3, P1, K2.
ROW 10: K3, P9, K3.
ROW 11: K2, P1, K3, sl 1, K2tog, psso, K3, P1, K2.
ROW 12: Rep Row 8.
ROW 13: K2, P1, K2, sl 1, K2tog, psso, K2, P1, K2.
ROW 14: Rep Row 6.
ROW 15: K2, P1, K1, sl 1, K2tog, psso, K1, P1, K2.
ROW 16: Rep Row 4.
ROW 17: K2, P1, sl 1, K2tog, psso, P1, K2.
ROW 18: Rep Row 2.

ROWS 19–22: K.
Rep Rows 1–22 for length required.
BO/CO.

190 Leaf edging

 53

SPECIAL ABBREVIATION:

INC = increase by knitting into the front and back of indicated stitch.

CO 8 sts.
ROW 1: (RS) K5, YO, K1, YO, K2.
ROW 2: P6, inc into next st, K3.
ROW 3: K4, P1, K2, YO, K1, YO, K3.
ROW 4: P8, inc into next st, K4.
ROW 5: K4, P2, K3, YO, K1, YO, K4.
ROW 6: P10, inc into next st, K5.
ROW 7: K4, P3, K4, YO, K1, YO, K5.
ROW 8: P12, inc into next st, K6.
ROW 9: K4, P4, sl 1, K1, psso, K7, K2tog, K1.

ROW 10: P10, inc into next st, K7.
ROW 11: K4, P5, sl 1, K1, psso, K5, K2tog, K1.
ROW 12: P8, inc into next st, K2, P1, K5.
ROW 13: K4, P1, K1, P4, sl 1, K1, psso, K3, K2tog, K1.
ROW 14: P6, inc into next st, K3, P1, K5.
ROW 15: K4, P1, K1, P5, sl 1, K1, psso, K1, K2tog, K1.
ROW 16: P4, inc into next st, K4, P1, K5.
ROW 17: K4, P1, K1, P6, sl 1, K2tog, psso, K1.
ROW 18: P2tog, BO/CO 5 sts using P2tog st as BO/CO first st, P3, K4.

Rep Rows 1–18 for length required.
BO/CO.

191 Shell & lace edging

FOUNDATION CHAIN: Ch 12.

ROW 1: (RS) 4 dc/*tr* into 4th ch from hook, ch 3, sk 3 chs, 4 dc/*tr* into next ch, ch 3, sk 3 chs, 1 dc/*tr* into last ch, turn.

ROW 2: Ch 6, 4 dc/*tr* into first st of first 4 dc/*tr* group, ch 3, 4 dc/*tr* into first st of next group, turn.

ROW 3: Ch 3, 4 dc/*tr* into first st of first 4 dc/*tr* group, ch 3, 4 dc/*tr* into first st of next group, ch 3, 1 dc/*tr* into 3rd of ch-6, turn.
Rep Rows 2 & 3 for length required.
Fasten off yarn.

192 Deep ruffled edging

CO 24 sts.

ROW 1: (WS) K.

ROW 2: P20, turn, K20.

ROW 3: P20, K4.

ROW 4: K4, P20.

ROW 5: K20, turn, P20.

ROW 6: K.
Rep Rows 1–6 for length required.
BO/*CO*.

193 Albemarle edging

SPECIAL ABBREVIATION:

MP = make picot by working [2 dc/*tr*, ch 4, sl st into 4th ch from hook, 2 dc/*tr*] into same stitch.

FOUNDATION CHAIN: Work a multiple of 4 chains plus 2.

ROW 1: (RS) 1 sc/*dc* in 2nd ch from hook, 1 sc/*dc* in each ch to end, turn.

ROWS 2 & 3: Ch 1, 1 sc/*dc* into each sc/*dc* of previous row, turn.

ROW 4: Ch 1, 1 sc/*dc* into next sc/*dc*, *ch 3, sk next 3 sc/*dc*, 1 dc/*tr* into next sc/*dc*, 4 sc/*dc* into sp made by dc/*tr* just worked, 1 sc/*dc* into same sc/*dc* as last dc/*tr*; rep from * to end, turn.

ROW 5: Sk first sc/*dc*, sl st into each of next 4 sc/*dc*, ch 3, [1 dc/*tr*, ch 4, sl st into 4th ch from hook, 2 dc/*tr*] into same sc/*dc* as sl st just worked, *sk next ch-3 sp and next 4 sc/*dc*, MP in next sc/*dc*; rep from * to end. Fasten off yarn.

194 Folded edging

CO an even number of sts.

ROWS 1 & 5: K.

ROWS 2, 4 & 6: P.

ROW 3: K2, *YO, K2tog; rep from * to end.

ROW 7: Fold work at Row 3 to make hem and knit together one st from needle and corresponding loop from CO edge.

ROWS 8–12: K.

BO/*CO*.

195 Royal edging

FOUNDATION CHAIN: Work a multiple of 5 chains plus 2.

ROW 1: (WS) 1 sc/*dc* into 2nd ch from hook, 1 sc/*dc* into each ch to end, turn.

ROW 2: Ch 1, 1 sc/*dc* into next sc/*dc*, *ch 5, sk next 4 sc/*dc*, 1 sc/*dc* into next sc/*dc*; rep from * to end.

ROW 3: Ch 1, 1 sc/*dc* into next sc/*dc*, ch 2, *5 dc/*tr* into next ch-5 sp, ch 2; rep from * to last sc/*dc*, 1 sc/*dc* into last sc/*dc*, turn.

ROW 4: Ch 1, 2 sc/*dc* into next ch-2 sp, *ch 5, 2 sc/*dc* into next ch-2 sp; rep from * to last sc/*dc*, 1 sc/*dc* into last sc/*dc*, turn.

ROW 5: Ch 1, sl st into next ch-5 sp, ch 1, 2 sc/*dc* into same ch-5 sp, *ch 6, sl st into 5th ch from hook, [ch 5, sl st into 5th ch from hook] twice, ch 1, 2 sc/*dc* into next ch-5 sp; rep from * to end. Fasten off yarn.

196 Wavy lace edging

CO 20 sts.

ROW 1: (RS) K.

ROW 2: Sl 1, K3, [YO, K2tog] 7 times, YO, K2.

ROWS 3, 5, 7 & 9: Rep Row 1.

ROW 4: Sl 1, K6, [YO, K2tog] 6 times, YO, K2.

ROW 6: Sl 1, K9, [YO, K2tog] 5 times, YO, K2.

ROW 8: Sl 1, K12, [YO, K2tog] 4 times, YO, K2.

ROW 10: Sl 1, K23.

ROW 11: BO/*CO* 4 sts, K19. Rep Rows 2–11 for length required. BO/*CO*.

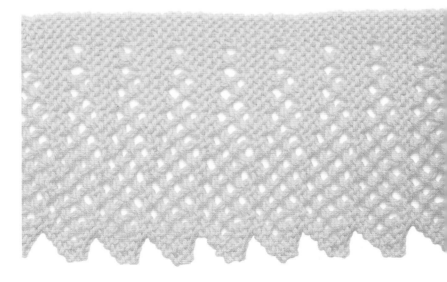

197 Edwardian edging

FOUNDATION ROW: Ch 20.

ROW 1: (RS) 1 dc/*tr* into 7th ch from hook, [ch 1, sk next ch, 1 dc/*tr* into next ch] twice, 2 dc/*tr* into each of next 2 chs, [1 dc/*tr* into next ch, ch 1, sk next ch] three times, 1 dc/*tr* into last ch, turn.

ROW 2: Ch 7, 1 dc/*tr* into first ch-1 sp, [ch 1, 1 dc/*tr* into next ch-1 sp] twice, ch 4, [1 dc/*tr* into next ch-1 sp, ch 1] twice, 1 dc/*tr* into top st of turning ch, 1 dc/*tr* into next ch, turn.

ROW 3: Ch 4, [1 dc/*tr* into next ch-1 sp, ch 1] twice, 6 dc/*tr* into ch-4 sp, [ch 1, 1 dc/*tr* into next ch-1 sp] twice, ch 1, 12 dc/*tr* into ch-7 sp at end of row and secure with sl st into last st of foundation ch, turn.

ROW 4: Ch 5, 1 sc/*dc* into 2nd st, [ch 5, sk next st, 1 sc/*dc* into next st] five times, ch 1, [1 dc/*tr* into next ch-1 sp, ch 1] twice, 1 dc/*tr* into next ch-1 sp, ch 4, [1 dc/*tr* into next ch-1 sp, ch 1] twice, 1 dc/*tr* into top st of turning ch, 1 dc/*tr* into next ch, turn.

ROW 5: Ch 4, [1 dc/*tr* into next ch-1 sp, ch 1] twice, 6 dc/*tr* into ch-4 sp, ch 1, [1 dc/*tr* into next ch-1 sp, ch 1] twice, 1 dc/*tr* into first of ch-5, turn.

ROW 6: Ch 7, 1 dc/*tr* into first ch-1 sp, [ch 1, 1 dc/*tr* into next ch-1 sp] twice, ch 4, [1 dc/*tr* into next ch-1 sp, ch 1] twice, 1 dc/*tr* into top st of turning ch, 1 dc/*tr* into next ch, turn.

ROW 7: Ch 4, [1 dc/*tr* into next ch-1 sp, ch 1] twice, 6 dc/*tr* into ch-4 sp, [ch 1, 1 dc/*tr* into next ch-1 sp] twice, ch 1, 12 dc/*tr* into ch-7 sp at end of row and secure with sl st into first of ch-5 where dc/*tr* was previously worked, turn.

ROW 8: Ch 5, 1 sc/*dc* into 2nd st, [ch 5, sk next st, 1 sc/*dc* into next st] five times, ch 1, [1 dc/*tr* into next ch-1 sp, ch 1] twice, 1 dc/*tr* into next ch-1 sp, ch 4, [1 dc/*tr* into next ch-1 sp, ch 1] twice, 1 dc/*tr* into top st of turning ch, 1 dc/*tr* into next ch, turn.

Repeat Rows 5–8 for length required.

Fasten off yarn.

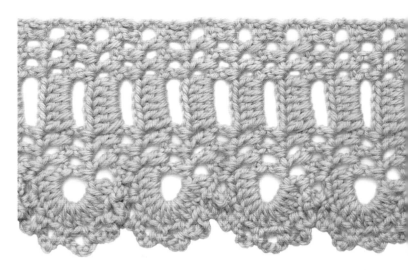

198 Branching edging

NOTE: Number of purl stitches worked on odd-numbered rows will vary.

CO 13 sts.

ROW 1 AND EVERY FOLL ALT ROW: (WS) K2, P to last 2 sts, K2.

ROW 2: Sl 1, K3, YO, K5, YO, K2tog, YO, K2.

ROW 4: Sl 1, K4, sl 1, K2tog, psso, K2, [YO, K2tog] twice, K1.

ROW 6: Sl 1, K3, sl 1, K1, psso, K2, [YO, K2tog] twice, K1.

ROW 8: Sl 1, K2, sl 1, K1, psso, K2, [YO, K2tog] twice, K1.

ROW 10: Sl 1, K1, sl 1, K1, psso, K2, [YO, K2tog] twice, K1.

ROW 12: K1, sl 1, K1, psso, K2, YO, K1, YO, K2tog, YO, K2.

ROW 14: Sl 1, [K3, YO] twice, K2tog, YO, K2.

Repeat Rows 1–14 for length required.

BO/*CO*.

199 Richelieu edging

FOUNDATION CHAIN: Ch 36.

ROW 1: (RS) 1 dc/*tr* into 4th ch from hook, ch 1, sk next ch, 1 dc/*tr* into each of next 2 chs, ch 1, sk next 3 chs, 3 dc/*tr* into next ch, ch 3, 3 dc/*tr* into next ch, [ch 1, sk next 5 chs, 3 dc/*tr* into next ch, ch 3, 3 dc/*tr* into next ch] three times, leave last 3 chs unworked, turn.

ROW 2: Ch 6, [1 dc/*tr*, ch 3, 1 dc/*tr*] into ch-3 sp, [ch 5, (1 dc/*tr*, ch 3, 1 dc/*tr*) into next ch-3 sp] three times, ch 3, sk next 3 dc/*tr*, 1 dc/*tr* into each of next 2 dc/*tr*, ch 1, 1 dc/*tr* into last dc/*tr*, 1 dc/*tr* into 3rd of beg skipped ch-3, turn.

ROW 3: Ch 3, 1 dc/*tr* into next dc/*tr*, ch 1, 1 dc/*tr* into each of next 2 dc/*tr*, [ch 1, (3 dc/*tr*, ch 3, 3 dc/*tr*) into next ch-3 sp] four times, [ch 1, 1 dc/*tr*] seven times into ch-6 sp, sl st into last ch of foundation chain, turn.

ROW 4: [Ch 3, 1 sc/*dc* into next ch-1 sp] seven times, ch 3, [1 dc/*tr*, ch 3, 1 dc/*tr*] into next ch-3 sp, [ch 5, (1 dc/*tr*, ch 3, 1 dc/*tr*) into next ch-3 sp] three times, ch 3, sk next 3 dc/*tr*, 1 dc/*tr* into each of next 2 dc/*tr*, ch 1, 1 dc/*tr* into next dc/*tr*, 1 dc/*tr* into 3rd of ch-3, turn.

ROW 5: Ch 3, 1 dc/*tr* into next dc/*tr*, ch 1, 1 dc/*tr* into each of next 2 dc/*tr*, [ch 1, (3 dc/*tr*, ch 3, 3 dc/*tr*) into next ch-3 sp] four times, turn.

ROW 6: Ch 6, [1 dc/*tr*, ch 3, 1 dc/*tr*] into ch-3 sp, [ch 5, (1 dc/*tr*, ch 3, 1 dc/*tr*) into next ch-3 sp] three times, ch 3, sk next 3 dc/*tr*, 1 dc/*tr* into each of next 2 dc/*tr*, ch 1, 1 dc/*tr* into last dc/*tr*, 1 dc/*tr* into 3rd of ch-3, turn.

ROW 7: Ch 3, 1 dc/*tr* into next dc/*tr*, ch 1, 1 dc/*tr* in each of next 2 dc/*tr*, [ch 1, (3 dc/*tr*, ch 3, 3 dc/*tr*) into next ch-3 sp] four times, [ch 1, 1 dc/*tr*] seven times into ch-6 sp, sl st into ch-3 sp of previous repeat, turn.

Rep Rows 4–7 for length required. Fasten off yarn.

200 Arrow edging

  57

CO 21 sts.

ROW 1: (RS) K3, YO, K2tog, P2, YO, sl 1, K1, psso, K3, K2tog, YO, P2, K1, YO, K2tog, K2.

ROWS 2 & 4: K3, YO, K2tog tbl, K2, P7, K3, YO, K2tog tbl, K2.

ROW 3: K3, YO, K2tog, P2, K1, YO, sl 1, K1, psso, K1, K2tog, YO, K1, P2, K1, YO, K2tog, K2.

ROW 5: K3, YO, K2tog, P2, K2, YO, sl 1, K2tog, psso, YO, K2, P2, K1, YO, K2tog, K2.

ROW 6: K3, YO, K2tog tbl, K2, P7, K3, YO, K2tog tbl, K2.

Rep Rows 1–6 for length required. BO/*CO*.

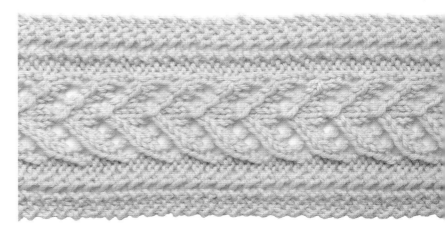

TECHNIQUES

In this chapter you will find a refresher course to help you make the blocks and stitch patterns shown in the directory, including tips on working seams and making a fringe. There are also details of the actual yarns used to work the swatches.

Knitting techniques

Knitting techniques are based on two simple stitches: the knit stitch and the purl stitch. Once you get the hang of casting on, working the basic stitches and binding/*casting* off, it is easy to move on to more complex techniques.

Before you begin it is worth noting that there is no right or wrong way to hold the yarn and needles, so choose the way that feels the most natural and comfortable to you.

Making a slip knot

The first step in knitting is to cast the required number of stitches on to one needle. First, you need to make a slip knot in the yarn, about 15cm (6in) away from the end of the yarn, and put the loop of the knot on to a needle.

1 Coil the yarn into a loop as shown. Insert the needle underneath the bottom strand and bring it forwards.

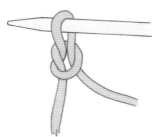

2 Gently pull one end of the yarn to tighten the knot, then pull the other end of the yarn to bring the knot close to the needle.

Casting on

This method of casting on, the cable cast-on, makes a neat, strong edge. If you find that your cast-on edge is too tight and pulls across the lower edge of the work, simply substitute a larger size of needle for the left needle, cast on, then change to the correct needle size on the next row.

1 Take the needle with the slip knot in your left hand. Insert the tip of the right needle into the front of the slip loop, take the yarn around the right needle and pull a stitch through. Transfer the stitch to the left needle.

2 From this point, insert the right needle between the stitches, take the yarn around the needle and pull a stitch through. Transfer each new stitch on to the left needle. Repeat until you have cast on the required number of stitches.

Working the basic stitches

There are two basic stitches in knitting: the knit stitch and the purl stitch. To make a row of stitches, work into each stitch on the left needle until they have all been transferred to the right needle. Then move the needle with the stitches to your left hand, ready to work the next row.

Making a knit stitch

If you knit every stitch of every row, the result is called garter stitch, and it looks exactly the same on both sides of the work.

1 Hold the needle with the cast-on stitches in your left hand. Insert the tip of the right needle into the front of the first stitch on the left needle from right to left.

2 Take the yarn behind both needles and pull a loop of yarn through to make a new stitch on the right needle. Slip the old stitch off the left needle.

Making a purl stitch

Purl stitches are the opposite of knit stitches. The best known combination of knit and purl stitches is called stockinette/*stocking* stitch, which is made by knitting and purling alternate rows. Knit rows form the smooth right side of stockinette/*stocking* stitch, and the purl rows form the ridged wrong side.

1 Holding yarn and needles in the same way as for working knit stitches, insert the tip of the right needle into the front of the first stitch from right to left.

2 Bring the yarn to the front and loop it around the tip of the right needle. Use the tip of the right needle to draw a loop of yarn through to make a new stitch on the right needle. Slip the old stitch off the left needle. Repeat.

Binding/*casting* off

When your knitting has reached the correct length, you need to finish off the last row to ensure the stitches do not unravel. This is called binding/*casting* off. If your bound/*cast* off edge is too tight, use a larger size needle for the right needle.

 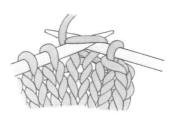

1 Knit the first two stitches. Insert the tip of the left needle into the first stitch on the right needle and lift it over the second stitch and off the right needle.

2 One stitch now remains on the right needle. Knit the next stitch on the left needle, insert the left needle into the first stitch on the right needle and repeat as before. Repeat along the whole row. Cut the yarn, leaving a tail of about 15cm (6in), and pull the tail through the stitch remaining on the right needle.

Joining new yarn

When you come close to the end of a ball of yarn, always plan to join new yarn into the knitting at the beginning or end of a row, to avoid unsightly joins in the middle of your work.

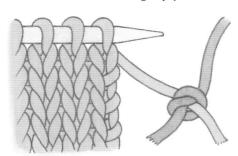

Tie the end of the new yarn loosely around the old yarn, leaving a tail of about 15cm (6in). Gently tighten the knot and slip it up the old yarn until it rests against the needle. Untie the knot later and weave the ends into the edge of the knitting.

Working into the back of stitches

The front of each stitch is always the loop closest to you, whether working right- or wrong-side rows. Unless stated in the pattern instructions, always work into the front loop of the stitch. When instructed to work into the back loop, work knit and purl stitches as shown below.

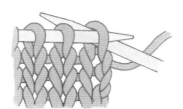 

1 **KNIT INTO THE BACK** To knit into the back loop of a stitch, insert the tip of the right needle under the left needle and into the loop of the stitch farthest from you, then knit this loop in the usual way.

2 **PURL INTO THE BACK** To purl into the back loop of a stitch, insert the tip of the right needle from back to front into the loop farthest from you, and purl this loop.

Slipping stitches

Many patterns tell you to slip one or more stitches. This is done by passing the stitches across from the left to the right needle without actually working them. Unless instructed otherwise, slip all stitches knitwise.

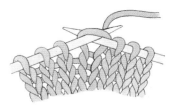

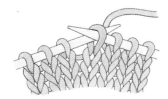

1 **SLIP KNITWISE** To slip a stitch knitwise, insert the tip of the right needle into the next stitch on the left needle as if you were knitting the stitch. Pull this stitch off the left needle. The stitch is now on the right needle.

2 **SLIP PURLWISE** To slip a stitch purlwise, insert the tip of the right needle into the next stitch on the left needle as if you were purling the stitch. Pull this stitch off the left needle. The stitch is now on the right needle.

Working increases and decreases

Increases and decreases alter the number of stitches on the needle in any given row, and they are used in knitting lace patterns.

Working a bar increase

Often worked on the knit side of the work, this is an easy increase made by simply knitting into the front and back of the same stitch. This type of increase can also be worked by purling twice into the same stitch.

1 Insert the tip of the right needle into the stitch to be increased as if you were going to knit it. Take the yarn around the needle and knit the stitch but do not slip it off the left needle.

2 Insert the right needle into the back of the same stitch, take the yarn around the needle and pull it through to make a second stitch. Slip the original stitch off the left needle.

Working a make one increase

This increase is less visible than the bar increase. One extra stitch is worked into the horizontal strand of yarn between two ordinary stitches.

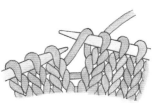

1 Insert the right needle from front to back under the strand between the last stitch worked and the first stitch on the left needle. Place it on the left needle.

2 Knit this strand through the back loop and slip the loop off the left needle to leave a new stitch on the right needle.

Working yarn overs

A yarn over is a decorative increase used in working lace patterns. It is made by wrapping the yarn around the right needle in various ways, depending on where the yarn over is placed in the instructions.

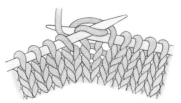

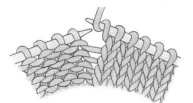

1 **BETWEEN TWO KNIT STITCHES** Bring the yarn between the needles from the back to the front of the work. Knit the next stitch, taking the yarn to the back over the right needle.

2 **BETWEEN A KNIT AND PURL STITCH** Bring the yarn between the needles from back to front. Take it back over the right needle and then to the front again. Purl the next stitch.

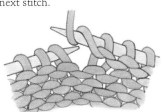

3 **BETWEEN A PURL AND KNIT STITCH** Leave the yarn at the front of the work. Knit the next stitch, taking the yarn to the back over the right needle.

4 **BETWEEN TWO PURL STITCHES** Leave the yarn at the front of the work. Take it to the back over the right needle and then to the front again. Purl the next stitch.

Working a single decrease

This method of decreasing one stitch at a time is usually worked on the right side of the work. Take care to slip stitches knitwise, to avoid the stitches becoming twisted. You can also knit two stitches together before passing the slip stitch over, reducing the stitches by two at a time.

1 **SLIP, KNIT, PASS STITCH OVER** Slip the next stitch knitwise from the left needle to the right needle, then knit the following stitch in the usual way. Insert the tip of the left needle into the front of the slipped stitch. Lift the slipped stitch over the knit stitch and off the right needle. One stitch has been decreased.

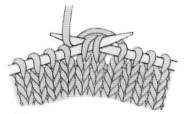

2 **SLIP, SLIP, KNIT (SSK)** The slip, slip, knit (ssk) single decrease is similar in appearance to the one on the left. Slip the next two stitches knitwise, one at a time, on to the right needle. Insert the tip of the left needle into the front of the two slipped stitches and knit them together. One stitch has been decreased.

Working two or more stitches together

Knitting or purling two stitches together is the simplest way of decreasing one stitch at a time. Usually, the knit version is used on right-side rows and the purl version on wrong-side rows. You can also work three stitches together in the same way.

1 **KNIT TWO TOGETHER (K2TOG)** To knit two stitches together, insert the right needle from front to back into the next two stitches on the left needle as if you were going to knit. Take the yarn around the needle and pull through to decrease one stitch.

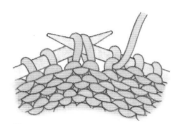

2 **PURL TWO TOGETHER (P2TOG)** To purl two stitches together, insert the right needle into the front loops of the next two stitches on the left needle as if you were going to purl. Take the yarn around the needle and pull through to decrease one stitch.

Working intarsia patterns

Intarsia is a multicoloured knitting technique worked row by row from a chart. The chart shows the pattern as a series of coloured squares, and each square represents one stitch. Work upwards from the bottom right-hand corner of the chart, reading odd-numbered rows (right-side knit rows) from right to left and even-numbered rows (wrong-side purl rows) from left to right.

Intarsia patterns have solid areas of colour; any number of colours can be used in one row and each area is worked with a separate length of yarn. For large and medium-sized colour areas, wind separate small balls of each yarn or wind the yarns on to plastic bobbins. For small areas, simply cut lengths of yarn and let them dangle freely at the back of the knitting. To stop holes from forming where colour areas meet, twist the yarns around each other at each colour change, as shown.

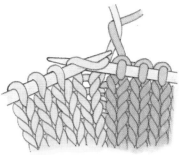

1 **KNIT ROW** To change colour on a knit (right-side) row, drop the old colour. Pick up the new colour from beneath the old colour and knit along the row to the next colour change.

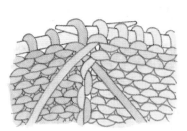

2 **PURL ROW** To change colour on a purl (wrong-side) row, drop the old colour. Pick up the new yarn from beneath the old colour and purl along the row to the next colour change.

Joining knitted blocks

Knitted blocks are joined by sewing them together with matching yarn, using one of the methods shown below. Always block (see page 124) the pieces before joining, and use the same weight of yarn for joining as was used for working the blocks. Begin by laying out the blocks in the correct order, with the right or wrong side of each one facing upwards, depending on the joining method you have chosen. Working first in horizontal rows, join the blocks together, beginning with the top row. Repeat until all the horizontal edges are joined. Turn the work so the remaining edges of the blocks are horizontal and, as before, join these edges together.

Working a backstitch seam

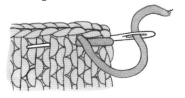 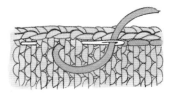

1 Hold the blocks to be joined with right sides together, pinning if necessary. Using matching yarn threaded in a yarn needle, secure the end of the seam by taking the needle twice around the edges from front to back. Bring out the needle a short distance away.

2 Insert the needle at the point where the yarn emerges from the previous stitch and bring it out a short distance in front. Pull the yarn through to complete the stitch and repeat along the edge.

 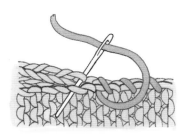

Working mattress stitch

Lay out the blocks with the right sides facing upwards and edges touching. Using matching yarn threaded in a yarn needle, weave around the centres of the stitches as shown, without pulling the stitches too tightly. Work in the same way when joining row ends.

Overcasting

Hold the blocks to be joined with right sides together, pinning if necessary. Using matching yarn threaded in a yarn needle, work a row of diagonal stitches from back to front, going through the strands at the edges of the blocks.

Couching

Couching is a linear embroidery stitch that works well on either knit or crochet fabric. Bring a length of yarn through to the right side and take a long stitch across the fabric, bringing the yarn back to the right side close to the end of the stitch. Secure the long stitch to the fabric by making a series of tiny straight stitches over it. You can work couching from left to right, as shown, or from right to left depending on your preference.

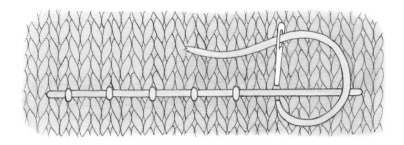

Crochet techniques

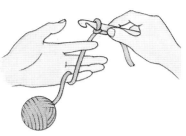

Crochet techniques are based on several simple stitches, each of a different height. Crochet can be worked in rows, beginning with a foundation chain, or in rounds working outwards from a foundation ring of chain stitches. Practise making chains and working the basic stitches before moving on to more challenging techniques.

Making a slip knot

1 Loop the yarn as shown, insert the hook into the loop, catch the yarn with the hook and pull it through to make a loop over the hook.

2 Gently pull the yarn to tighten the loop around the hook and complete the slip knot.

Holding the hook and yarn

The most common way of holding the hook is shown below, but if this does not feel comfortable to you, try grasping the flat section of the hook between your thumb and forefinger as if you were holding a knife.

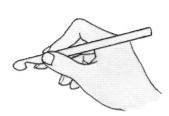

1 Holding the hook as if it were a pen is the most widely used method. Centre the tips of your right thumb and forefinger over the flat section of the hook.

2 To control the supply and keep an even tension on the yarn, loop the short end of the yarn over your left forefinger and take the yarn coming from the ball loosely around the little finger on the same hand. Use your middle finger on the same hand to help hold the work. If you are left-handed, hold the hook in your left hand and the yarn in your right.

Working a foundation chain

The foundation chain is the equivalent of casting on in knitting, and it is important to make sure that you have made the required number of chains for the pattern you are going to work. Count each V-shaped loop on the front of the chain as one chain stitch, except for the loop on the hook, which is not counted. When working the first row of stitches into the chain, insert the hook under one thread or two, depending on your preference.

1 Holding the hook with the slip knot in your right hand and the yarn in your left, wrap the yarn over the hook. Draw the yarn through to make a new loop and complete the first chain stitch.

2 Repeat this step, drawing a new loop of yarn through the loop already on the hook until the chain is the required length. After every few stitches move up your thumb and forefinger, which are grasping the chain, to keep the tension even.

Turning and starting chains

When working crochet in rows or rounds, you will need to work a specific number of extra chains at the beginning of each row or round. When the work is turned at the end of a straight row, the extra chains are called a turning chain, and when they are worked at the beginning of a round, they are called a starting chain.

The extra chains are needed to bring the hook up to the correct height for the particular stitch you will be working next. The turning or starting chain is usually counted as the first stitch of the row or round, except when working single/*double* crochet where the turning chain is ignored. A chain may be longer than the number required for the stitch, and in that case counts as one stitch plus a number of chains. At the end of the row or round, the final stitch is usually worked into the top chain of the turning or starting chain or into another specified stitch of the chain.

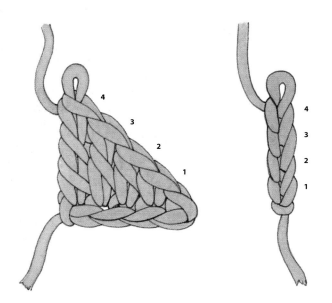

The illustrations above show the usual number of chain stitches that are worked to form the turning or starting chain for each stitch.

SINGLE/*DOUBLE* **CROCHET** – 1 chain
HALF DOUBLE/*TREBLE* **CROCHET** – 2 chains
DOUBLE/*TREBLE* **CROCHET** – 3 chains
TREBLE/*DOUBLE TREBLE* **CROCHET** – 4 chains

Slip stitch

Slip stitch is the shortest of all the crochet stitches and its main uses are for joining stitches and carrying the hook and yarn from one place to another.

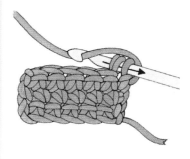

Insert the hook from front to back into the required stitch. Wrap the yarn over the hook and draw it through both the work and the loop on the hook. One loop remains on the hook and one slip stitch has been worked.

Single/*double* crochet

1 Begin with a foundation chain and insert the hook from front to back into the second chain from the hook. Wrap the yarn over the hook and draw it through the first loop, leaving two loops on the hook.

2 To complete the stitch, wrap the yarn over the hook and draw it through both loops on the hook, leaving one loop on the hook. Continue in this way, working one stitch into each chain.

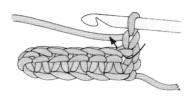

3 At the end of the row, turn and work one chain for the turning chain (remember that this chain does not count as a stitch). Insert the hook into the first single/*double* crochet at the beginning of the row. Work a single/*double* crochet into each stitch of the previous row, being careful to work the final stitch into the last stitch of the row, not into the turning chain.

Half double/*treble* crochet

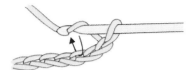

1 Begin with a foundation chain. Wrap the yarn over the hook and insert the hook into the third chain from the hook.

2 Draw the yarn through the chain, leaving three loops. Wrap the yarn over the hook and draw through all three loops on the hook, leaving one loop on the hook.

3 Continue along the row, working one stitch into each chain. At the end of the row, work two chains to turn. Skip the first stitch and work a half double/*treble* crochet into each stitch made on the previous row. At the end of the row, work the last stitch into the top of the turning chain.

Double/*treble* crochet

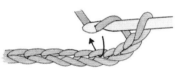

1 Begin with a foundation chain, then wrap the yarn over the hook and insert the hook into the fourth chain from the hook.

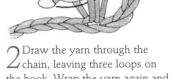

2 Draw the yarn through the chain, leaving three loops on the hook. Wrap the yarn again and draw the yarn through the first two loops on the hook, leaving two loops on the hook.

3 Wrap the yarn over the hook and draw it through the two loops on the hook, leaving one loop on the hook. Repeat along the row. At the end of the row, work three chains to turn. Skip the first stitch and work a double/*treble* crochet into each stitch. At the end of the row, work the last stitch into the top of the turning chain.

Treble/*double treble* crochet

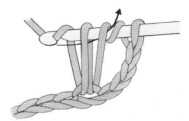

1 Begin with a foundation chain. Wrap the yarn over the hook twice and insert the hook into the fifth chain from the hook.

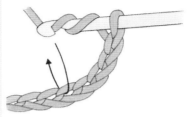

2 Draw the yarn through the chain, leaving four loops on the hook. Wrap the yarn again and draw the yarn through the first two loops on the hook, leaving three loops on the hook.

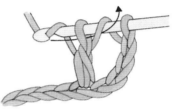

3 Wrap the yarn again and draw through the first two loops on the hook, leaving two loops on the hook.

4 Wrap the yarn again and draw through the two remaining loops, leaving one loop on the hook. Continue along the row, working one stitch into each chain. At the end of the row, work four chains to turn. Skip the first stitch and work a treble/*double treble* crochet into each stitch made on the previous row. At the end of the row, work the last stitch into the top of the turning chain.

Joining new yarn

Some of the instructions in the book, especially for blocks worked in the round, will tell you exactly where to join the next yarn.

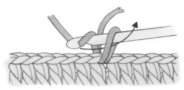 

1 **JOIN YARN B TO ANY DC**/*TR* The instruction 'Join yarn B to any dc/tr', means that you should join the next yarn colour to any of the double/*treble* crochet stitches worked on the previous round. To do this, insert the hook in the work as instructed and draw up a loop of the new colour, leaving a tail of about 10cm (4in). Work one chain and continue with the new yarn.

2 **JOIN YARN B** When instructed to 'Join yarn B' without being given a specific position, you should join the new yarn where the old one ends. To do this in the middle of a row or at the end of a row, leave the last stitch of the old colour incomplete so there are two loops on the hook and wrap the new colour around the hook.

3 Draw the new colour through to complete the stitch and continue working in the new colour. The illustrations show a colour change in a row of double/*treble* crochet stitches; the method is the same for the other stitches.

Fastening off yarn

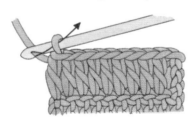

To fasten off the yarn, cut the yarn 15cm (6in) from the last stitch and pull the yarn end through the loop on the hook. Gently pull the yarn end to tighten the loop. To finish off yarn ends, thread the end in a yarn needle and weave the end through several stitches on the wrong side of the work. Trim the remaining yarn.

Working clusters

Clusters are decorative stitches made by working multiples of single/*double*, half double/*treble*, double/*treble* or treble/*double treble* crochet stitches. The last loop of each stitch forming the cluster remains on the hook until they are worked together at the end. When working a beginning cluster, count the turning or starting chain as the first stitch.

1 To work a three double/*treble* crochet cluster, work the first stitch, omitting the last stage to leave two loops on the hook. Work the second and third stitches in the same way, leaving the last loop of each stitch on the hook. You now have four loops on the hook.

2 Draw the yarn through all four loops to complete the cluster and secure the stitches.

Working popcorns

A popcorn is a group of double/*treble* crochet stitches (the number may vary) sharing the same base stitch, which is folded and closed at the top so the popcorn is raised from the background stitches.

1 To make a popcorn with four stitches, work a group of four double/*treble* crochet stitches into the same place.

2 Take the hook out of the working loop and insert it under both loops of the first double/*treble* crochet in the group. Pick up the working loop with the hook and draw it through to fold the group of stitches and close it at the top.

Working bobbles

A bobble is a group of between three and six double/*treble* crochet stitches worked into the same stitch and closed at the top. Bobbles are worked on wrong-side rows and they are usually surrounded by shorter stitches to throw them into high relief. When working bobbles in a contrasting colour, use a separate length of yarn to make each bobble, carrying the main yarn across the back of the bobble.

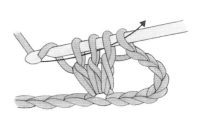

To make a three-stitch bobble, work three double/*treble* crochet stitches into the same stitch, omitting the last stage of each stitch so the last loop of each one remains on the hook. You now have four loops on the hook. Wrap the yarn over the hook and draw it through the four loops to secure them and complete the bobble.

Working decreases

One or two stitches can be decreased by working two or three incomplete stitches together, and the method is the same for single/*double*, half double/*treble*, double/*treble* or treble/*double treble* crochet stitches.

Decreasing by working two stitches together (dc2tog/*tr2tog*)

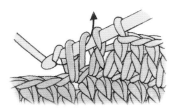

1 Leave the first stitch incomplete so there are two loops on the hook, then work another incomplete stitch so you have three loops on the hook.

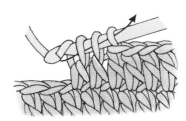

2 Wrap the yarn and draw through all three loops to finish the decrease. Two stitches can be decreased in the same way by working three stitches together. When working in double/*treble* crochet, this decrease is called dc3tog/*tr3tog*.

Working filet crochet

Filet crochet charts are numbered at the sides. Follow the numbered sequence, working upwards from the bottom and from side to side. Read odd-numbered (right-side) rows from right to left of the chart and even-numbered (wrong-side) rows from left to right.

Each open square on a chart represents one space. A space is made by working two double/*treble* crochet separated by two chains. When a square on the chart is filled in, the chains are replaced by two double/*treble* crochet to make a solid block of four stitches. Two blocks together on the chart are filled by seven stitches, three blocks by ten stitches and so on.

Charts begin with the first row, so the foundation chain is not shown. To calculate this, multiply the number of squares across the chart by three and add one. For example, for a chart that is 20 squares across, make a foundation chain 61 chains long ($20 \times 3 + 1$). You also need to add the correct number of turning chains, depending on whether the first chart row begins with a space or a block (see below).

Working the first row

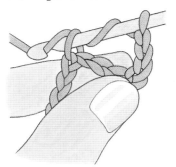

1 **STARTING THE FIRST ROW WITH A SPACE** Make the foundation chain, calculating the number of chains as described above. Start to follow the chart from the bottom right-hand corner, along the row of squares marked 1. When the first square is a space, add four turning chains and work the first double/*treble* crochet stitch into the eighth chain from the hook. Continue working spaces and blocks along the row, reading the chart from right to left.

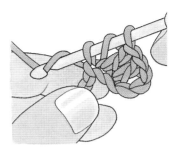

2 **STARTING THE FIRST ROW WITH A BLOCK** When the first square on the chart is a block, add two turning chains and work the first double/*treble* crochet stitch into the fourth chain from the hook. Work one double/*treble* crochet stitch into each of the next two chains to complete the first block. Continue along the row, reading the chart from right to left.

Working the rest of the chart rows

At the end of the first row, turn the work and follow the second row of the chart, reading from left to right. Work spaces and blocks at the beginning and end of the second and subsequent rows as follows.

1 **WORKING A SPACE OVER A SPACE ON THE PREVIOUS ROW** At the beginning of a row, work five turning chains (counts as one double/*treble* crochet stitch and two chains), skip the first stitch and the next two chains, work one double/*treble* crochet stitch into the next double/*treble* crochet stitch, then continue working the spaces and blocks from the chart.

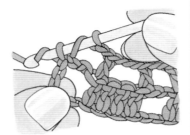

2 At the end of a row, finish with one double/*treble* crochet stitch into the last double/*treble* crochet stitch, work two chains, skip two chains, work one double/*treble* crochet stitch into the third of five chains, turn.

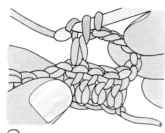

3 **WORKING A SPACE OVER A BLOCK ON THE PREVIOUS ROW** At the beginning of the row, work five turning chains (counts as one double/*treble* crochet stitch and two chains), skip the first three stitches, work one double/*treble* crochet stitch into the next double/*treble* crochet stitch, then continue working spaces and blocks from the chart.

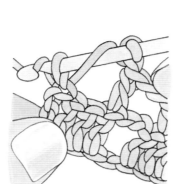

4 At the end of a row, work to the last four stitches. Work one double/*treble* crochet stitch into the next stitch, work two chains, skip two stitches, work one double/*treble* crochet stitch into the top of three chains to complete the block, turn.

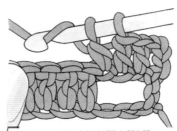

5 **WORKING A BLOCK OVER A SPACE ON THE PREVIOUS ROW** At the beginning of the row, work three turning chains (counts as one double/*treble* crochet stitch), skip one stitch, work one double/*treble* crochet stitch into each of the next two chains, and one double/*treble* crochet stitch into the next stitch to complete the block. Continue across the row working spaces and blocks from the chart.

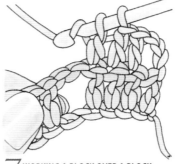

6 At the end of a row, finish with one double/*treble* crochet stitch into the last double/*treble* crochet stitch, one double/*treble* crochet stitch into each of the next three chains of the turning chain, turn.

7 **WORKING A BLOCK OVER A BLOCK ON THE PREVIOUS ROW** At the beginning of the row, work three turning chains (counts as one double/*treble* crochet stitch), skip one stitch, work one double/*treble* crochet stitch into each of the next three double/*treble* crochet stitches to complete the block. Continue across the row working spaces and blocks from the chart.

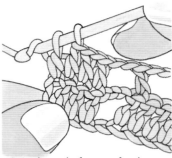

8 At the end of a row, finish with one double/*treble* crochet stitch into each of the last three double/*treble* crochet stitches, one double/*treble* crochet stitch into the top of three chains, turn.

Working in rounds

Blocks worked in rounds are worked outwards from a central ring of chains, called a foundation ring.

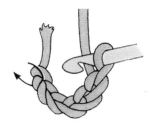

Making a foundation ring

Work a short length of foundation chain (see page 117) as specified in the pattern. Join the chains into a ring by working a slip stitch (see page 118) into the first stitch of the foundation chain.

Working into the ring

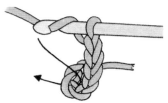

1 Work the number of starting chains specified in the pattern – three chains are shown here (counting as one double/*treble* crochet stitch). Inserting the hook into the space at the centre of the ring each time, work the number of stitches specified in the pattern.

2 Count the stitches at the end of the round to check that you have worked the correct number. Join the first and last stitches of the round together by working a slip stitch into the top (or other specified stitch) of the starting chain.

Finishing off the final round

1 Cut the yarn, leaving a tail of about 10cm (4in), and draw it through the last stitch. With right side facing, thread the tail in a yarn needle and take it under both loops of the stitch next to the starting chain.

2 Insert the needle into the centre of the last stitch of the round. On the wrong side, pull the needle through to complete the stitch, adjust the length of the stitch to close the round, then weave in the tail on the wrong side and trim.

Joining crochet blocks

Crochet blocks can be joined either by sewing or by crocheting them together with a hook. Always block (see page 124) the pieces before joining, and use the same weight of yarn for joining as you used for working the blocks. Begin by laying out the blocks in the correct order with the right or wrong side of each one facing upwards, depending on the joining method you have chosen. Working first in horizontal rows, join the blocks together, beginning with the top row. Repeat until all the horizontal edges are joined. Turn the work so the remaining edges of the blocks are horizontal and, as before, join these edges together.

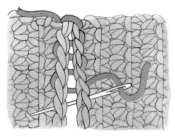

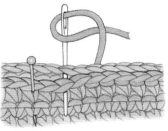

Working a woven seam

Lay the blocks out with the wrong sides facing upwards and edges touching. Using matching yarn threaded in a yarn needle, weave around the centres of the stitches as shown, without pulling the stitches too tightly. Work in the same way when joining row ends.

Working a backstitch seam

Hold the blocks to be joined with right sides together, pinning if necessary. Using matching yarn threaded in a yarn needle, work a row of evenly spaced backstitches (see page 116) close to the edge of the blocks.

Working a slip stitch seam

Joining blocks with the wrong sides together gives a firm seam with an attractive ridge on the right side. If you prefer not to see the ridge, join the blocks with right sides facing so the ridge is on the wrong side. Work a row of slip stitches (see page 118) through both loops of each block. When working this method along the side edges of blocks worked in rows, work enough evenly spaced stitches so the seam is not too tight.

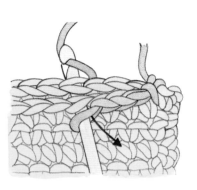

Finishing edges

You can work one or more rows of single/*double* crochet edging (see below) to finish off your crochet or knitted blanket. The edge finish will also make a good base for a yarn fringe, or you can insert the fringe directly into the edge of the knitted fabric.

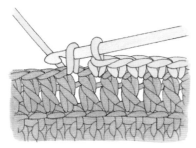 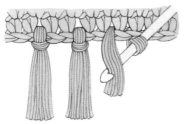

Working into the blanket edge

Single/*double* crochet edging is worked directly into crochet fabric and makes a neat, firm edge finish. To finish a blanket, work one or more rounds of single/*double* crochet right around the edge, changing the yarn colour on every round if you want to make a striped border. You can also edge knitted blankets with this edge finish.

Applying an edging

The decorative edgings shown on pages 98–111 are worked in rows either widthways or lengthways. Make the edging long enough to go around the edge of your blanket, allowing extra to gather or pleat around the corners so the edging will lay flat when it is attached. Pin the edging in place, making sure that the corners are neat. Choose a matching yarn colour and stitch or crochet the edging in place.

Making a fringe

Cut the yarn to twice the required length of the fringe plus about 5cm (2in) extra. Take four or more lengths of yarn and fold in half. Insert a large crochet hook through the knitted or crochet edge from back to front and draw the folded end of the yarn through to make a loop. Hook the ends through the loop and gently tighten the knot. Repeat at regular intervals along the edge, then trim the yarn ends evenly with sharp scissors.

Pressing and blocking

Finished pieces should be lightly pressed on the wrong side over a well-padded ironing board, with the iron temperature set according to the information given on the ball band of your yarn. Avoid pressing acrylic yarns because they will become limp and lifeless with too much heat.

Blocking involves pinning crochet or knit fabric out to the correct size, then either steaming it with an iron or moistening it with cold water, depending on the fibre content of your yarn. Always be guided by the information given on the ball band of your yarn and, when in doubt, choose the cold water blocking method.

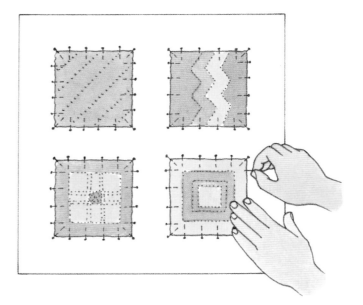

Before joining them, pin out the blocks to the correct size on a flat surface, such as an ironing board or a specialist blocking board, using rust-proof pins. To block woollen yarns with warm steam, hold a steam iron, set at the correct temperature for the yarn, about 2cm (¾in) above the surface of the block and allow the steam to penetrate for several seconds without allowing the iron to come into contact with the fabric. Lay the board flat and allow to dry before removing the pins.

To block acrylic and wool/acrylic blend yarns, pin out as above, then use a spray bottle to mist the item with clean cold water until it is evenly moist all over, but not saturated. Pat with your hand to help the moisture penetrate more easily. Lay the board flat and allow to dry completely before removing the pins.

Gauge/*tension*

Gauge/*tension* refers to the number of stitches and rows worked in a given area of either crochet or knit fabric, and these two numbers are usually quoted on the ball band of the yarn. Because no two people will crochet or knit to exactly the same gauge/*tension*, even working with the identical yarn and hook or needle sizes, you should always make a swatch before commencing a project. The swatch will allow you to compare your gauge/*tension* with the one in a pattern, if stated, and give you a good idea of how the finished fabric will feel and drape. It is also the ideal way to check how your chosen colours work together.

For stitch patterns

Work several centimetres or inches of at least two pattern repeats and press or block (see page 124). Using a ruler, measure how many stitches and rows you have made in a 10cm (4in) area at the centre of the swatch. If your measurements are smaller than required, make another swatch using a hook or needles one size larger. Also do this when the fabric feels tight and stiff. If your measurements are larger than required, make another swatch using a hook or needles one size smaller. Also do this if the fabric feels loose, stretchy and floppy. You may need to make several swatches using different sizes of hook or needles until you are happy with the gauge/*tension* and feel of your crochet or knit fabric.

For blocks

Each of the blocks in the book was worked by the author using the same weight of yarn – double knitting (DK) weight – and the same size of needles or hook – 4mm (US size 6) needles, 4mm (US size G) hook. No two people will knit or crochet to exactly the same gauge/*tension*, even when working with identical yarn and needles or hook. How you hold the needles or hook and the rate at which the yarn flows through your fingers will affect the gauge/*tension* you produce, so you may need to alter the needle or hook size to achieve the required gauge/*tension*.

Each of the blocks in the photographs measures 15cm (6in) square. To check your own gauge/*tension*, make a sample block using the same weight of yarn and the same needle or hook size. Measure the block. It should be slightly smaller than the stated size to allow for blocking (see page 124). If your block is smaller than required, make another sample using a size larger needle or hook. Also do this when the knitted or crochet fabric feels tight and hard. If your block is larger than required, make another sample using a size smaller needle or hook. Also do this when the fabric feels loose and floppy. Keep adjusting the needle or hook size until the block is the desired size and the fabric feels soft and pliable, but not too floppy.

Don't forget that you can work the blocks in any weight of yarn you choose. Using a finer yarn than double knitting weight and smaller needle/hook sizes will make the blocks smaller; heavier yarn and larger needle/hook sizes will produce larger blocks. There is a chart on page 9 giving suggested hook and needle sizes for use with a variety of different yarn weights.

Yarn list

When creating the swatches in this book, colours were chosen from a wide palette of over 60 shades of double knitting (DK) weight yarn and eight shades of 4ply (sport) weight yarn. Below you will find pictures of a small piece of the actual yarns used, arranged by colour.

1
WHITE *King Cole Merino DK, shade 'Snow White'*
SWATCHES 104, 146

2
CREAM *King Cole Merino DK, shade 'Cream'*
SWATCHES 21, 22, 103, 109, 112, 136, 142, 153

3
BUTTER *Jaeger Matchmaker DK, shade 727*
SWATCHES 1, 2, 21, 49, 50, 51, 120, 131, 132, 148

4
SUNSHINE YELLOW *King Cole Merino DK, shade 'Gold'*
SWATCHES 12, 45, 46, 58, 59, 65, 85, 87, 88, 117, 120, 149, 151 152, 157, 158, 159, 192, 196

5
MUSTARD *Debbie Bliss Merino DK, shade 504*
SWATCHES 2, 30, 34, 36, 40, 68, 101, 103, 104, 131

6
AMBER *King Cole Merino DK, shade 'Amber'*
SWATCHES 22, 24, 36, 40, 66, 133, 135, 136, 175

7
ORANGE *Jaeger Matchmaker DK, shade 898*
SWATCHES 36, 59, 66, 103

8
BURNT ORANGE *Jaeger Extra Fine Merino DK, shade 979*
SWATCHES 22, 23, 67, 134

9
SALMON *King Cole Merino DK, shade 'Salmon'*
SWATCHES 79, 94, 96, 142

10
PALE CORAL *Jaeger Matchmaker DK, shade 881*
SWATCHES 79, 93, 94, 95,198

11
BRIGHT CORAL *King Cole Merino DK, shade 'Bright Coral'*
SWATCHES 113, 114

12
DARK CORAL *Jaeger Matchmaker DK, shade 870*
SWATCHES 79, 80, 93, 94, 96, 199

13
CHERRY *Debbie Bliss Merino DK, shade 700*
SWATCHES 26, 27, 28, 48, 49, 85, 86, 87, 149, 150, 193

14
DARK RASPBERRY *Jaeger Extra Fine Merino DK, shade 943*
SWATCHES 26, 27, 28, 91

15
ELDERBERRY *Jaeger Extra Fine Merino DK, shade 944*
SWATCHES 26, 28

16
VARIEGATED PALE PINK *Jaeger Baby Merino DK, shade 212*
SWATCHES 13, 15, 61, 83, 106, 108, 124, 128, 163

17
BABY PINK *Jaeger Baby Merino DK, shade 221*
SWATCHES 14, 165

18
DAWN PINK *Jaeger Matchmaker DK, shade 883*
SWATCHES 41, 44, 122

19
CUPID PINK *Jaeger Extra Fine Merino DK, shade 989*
SWATCHES 42, 64, 99, 108, 162

20
CLOVER PINK *King Cole Merino DK, shade 'Dusky Pink'*
SWATCHES 15, 16, 43, 61, 63, 81, 105, 108, 114, 121, 123, 161

21
FUCHSIA *Jaeger Matchmaker DK, shade 896*
SWATCHES 6, 7, 8, 42, 57, 59, 61, 62, 74, 75, 108, 116, 143, 164, 177

22
LIGHT RASPBERRY *King Cole Merino DK, shade 'Raspberry'*
SWATCHES 25, 26, 27, 89, 106, 108, 123

23
VARIEGATED FUCHSIA *Jaeger Baby Merino DK, shade 193*
SWATCHES 61, 108, 124, 166

24
MAGENTA *Jaeger Matchmaker DK, shade 887*
SWATCHES 18, 19, 116, 142

25
AUBERGINE *Jaeger Matchmaker DK, shade 894*
SWATCHES 44, 123

26
PEARL *Jaeger Matchmaker DK, shade 891*
SWATCHES 9, 44, 53, 128

27
MAUVE *Jaeger Matchmaker DK, shade 882*
SWATCHES 44, 108, 126, 170

28
DEEP MAUVE *King Cole Merino DK, shade 'Mauve'*
SWATCHES 26, 53, 54, 108

29
PALE VIOLET *Jaeger Matchmaker DK, shade 893*
SWATCHES 167, 172

30
ANTIQUE VIOLET *Jaeger Matchmaker DK, shade 626*
SWATCHES 53, 108, 111

31
PALE LAVENDER *Jaeger Baby Merino DK, shade 224*
SWATCHES 44, 49, 51, 52, 53, 54, 56, 109, 111, 112, 153, 156, 169, 171

32
LAVENDER *Jaeger Matchmaker DK, shade 888*
SWATCHES 5, 6, 7, 17, 18, 36, 42, 44, 53, 54, 59, 74, 97, 100, 108, 110, 141, 143, 168, 173, 178

33
AMETHYST *Jaeger Matchmaker DK, shade 897*
SWATCHES 1, 18, 54

34

VARIEGATED PURPLE *Jaeger Baby Merino DK, shade 194*

SWATCHES 53, 112, 127

35

PUTTY *Jaeger Matchmaker DK, shade 892*

SWATCHES 1, 71, 139, 140, **149**

36

VARIEGATED PALE BLUE *Jaeger Baby Merino DK, shade 213*

SWATCHES 18, 156

37

SKY BLUE *Jaeger Matchmaker DK, shade 864*

SWATCHES 2, 4, 37, 49, 50, 81, 82, 109, 138, 153, 180

38

OCEAN BLUE *Jaeger Extra Fine Merino DK, shade 940*

SWATCHES 3, 18, 94, 96, 184

39

BLUEBELL *King Cole Merino DK, shade 'Bluebell'*

SWATCHES 1, 2, 6, 18, 26, 27, 39, 40, 59, 60, 69, 70, 74, 100, 139, 140, 179

40

LARKSPUR *King Cole Merino DK, shade 'Larkspur'*

SWATCHES 2, 19, 20, 37, 137, 140, 182

41

MARINER BLUE *Jaeger Matchmaker DK, shade 629*

SWATCHES 94, 96

42

ROYAL BLUE *King Cole Merino DK, shade 'Royal'*

SWATCHES 45, 85, 86, 140, 149, 150, 152, 191, 195

43

BLACKCURRANT *Jaeger Extra Fine Merino DK, shade 945*

SWATCH 140

44

PALE TURQUOISE *Jaeger Matchmaker DK, shade 884*

SWATCHES 51, 70, 71, 98, 99, 100, 140, 183

45

MID TURQUOISE *King Cole Merino DK, shade 'Turquoise'*

SWATCHES 6, 11, 12, 37, 38, 59, 70, 71, 72, 99, 115, 140, 159, 160, 176, 181

46

DEEP TURQUOISE *Jaeger Baby Merino DK, shade 226*

SWATCHES 9, 35, 36, 71, 99, 114, 157

47

VARIEGATED TURQUOISE *Jaeger Baby Merino DK, shade 192*

SWATCHES 9, 34

48

BRIGHT JADE *King Cole Merino DK, shade 'Green Ice'*

SWATCHES 6, 7, 59, 73, 74, 76

49

EMERALD *King Cole Merino DK, shade 'Emerald'*

SWATCHES 45, 48, 87, 149, 150, 189, 194

50

BALM *Jaeger Extra Fine Merino DK, shade 990*

SWATCHES 15, 19, 30, 61, 78, 81, 91, 130, 131, 145, 146, 153, 154

51

MINT GREEN *Jaeger Baby Merino DK, shade 223*

SWATCHES 49, 78, 80, 83, 92, 128, 130, 185

52

ASPARAGUS *Jaeger Matchmaker DK, shade 886*

SWATCHES 5, 6, 7, 57, 59, 73, 77, 78, 79, 90, 114, 116, 117, 119, 120, 130, 145, 147, 157, 159, 174, 186, 187

53

GRASS GREEN *Cygnet Superwash DK, shade 2817*

SWATCHES 30, 31, 32, 33, 36, 78, 117, 130, 145, 190

54

LINDEN GREEN *King Cole Merino DK, shade 'Linden'*

SWATCHES 63, 89, 129, 130, 131, 142, 143, 188

55

HOP *Jaeger Matchmaker DK, shade 899*

SWATCHES 30, 117, 118, 145

56

SAGE GREEN *Jaeger Matchmaker DK, shade 857*

SWATCHES 31, 79, 91, 130, 145

57

OATMEAL *Jaeger Matchmaker DK, shade 663*

SWATCHES 16, 23, 65, 66, 102, 104, 117, 200

58

SAND *King Cole Merino DK, shade 'Sand'*

SWATCHES 22, 37, 66, 67, 133, 134, 136

59

MUSHROOM *Jaeger Matchmaker DK, shade 880*

SWATCHES 66, 134

60

TOFFEE *Jaeger Matchmaker DK, shade 789*

SWATCHES 102, 104, 133, 134

61

SILVER GREY *King Cole Merino DK, shade 'Silver'*

SWATCHES 134, 197

62

GRANITE *Jaeger Matchmaker DK, shade 639*

SWATCH 133

63

SUGAR PINK *Jaeger Matchmaker 4ply, shade 694*

SWATCH 84

64

CUPID PINK *Jaeger Matchmaker 4ply, shade 742*

SWATCH 107

65

CERISE *Jaeger Matchmaker 4ply, shade 747*

SWATCH 144

66

PURPLE *Jaeger Matchmaker 4ply, shade 755*

SWATCH 55

67

PALE BLUE *Jaeger Matchmaker 4ply, shade 744*

SWATCH 155

68

HYACINTH BLUE *Jaeger Matchmaker 4ply, shade 650*

SWATCH 125

69

PETROL BLUE *Jaeger Matchmaker 4ply, shade 741*

SWATCH 10

70

LIGHT OLIVE *Jaeger Matchmaker 4ply, shade 715*

SWATCH 29

Index

Credits

The author would like to thank Liz Marley for knitting the beautiful baby blanket featured in the book. The knitted baby blanket is worked in stitch pattern 71 (Old shale, p53). The crochet baby blanket combines blocks 44 (Wagon wheel, p39), 57 (Colourful square, p46), 100 (Blue dahlia, p67) and 140 (Dotty p87).

Thanks also to Connor and Isabelle for modelling the baby blankets so well!

All photographs and illustrations are the copyright of Quarto Publishing plc. While every effort has been made to credit contributors, Quarto would like to apologise should there have been any omissions or errors – and would be pleased to make the appropriate correction for future editions of the book.

American terminology	English terminology
bind off	cast off
gauge	tension
stockinette stitch	stocking stitch
single crochet (sc)	double crochet (dc)
half double crochet (hdc)	half treble crochet (htr)
double crochet (dc)	treble crochet (tr)
treble crochet (tr)	double treble crochet (dtr)